RADIO RAT

TEAM SUZUKI
Arai
HELMET
GIGA
SNELL
FRANK
VINCENT

RADIO RAT

FRANK VINCENT

CONTENTS

Riding high — 25 storeys high on top of the world and my game as brand new announcer at the revolutionary 2 Triple M.

INTRODUCTION

Welcome to the wild world of radio's everywhere man.

The adventures of The Black Rat – AKA Frank Vincent – are utterly captivating and inspiring, as a boy from the burbs brushes shoulders with the biggest names on the planet in a broadcasting career spanning five decades.

From basketball god Michael Jordan to supermodel Claudia Schiffer and a galaxy of megastars in between Frank Vincent has seen, met and heard them all.

Radio Rat tracks his own stellar rise from the tough streets of western Sydney into the domains of the super famous as he lands on the red carpet, the studios and front row seats of the sporting and concert arenas that make up the world stage.

An original member of the Mulray Bunch – the most successful breakfast crew in Australian radio history – Frank takes the reader on a dizzying odyssey that charts the golden years of Australian rock n roll and the sublime achievements of the world's supreme athletes.

From the highs of covering soccer world cups and Olympic Games to the – literally – crippling impacts of vicious and ultimately vexatious accusations Frank Vincent spins a remarkable tale of a life that will challenge you not to read all about it in one sitting.

"Doors won't open if you don't knock on them. Doors won't open if you don't barge into them with a shoulder. Doors won't open unless you kick them in. Doors won't open unless you pick the lock."

- Frank Vincent, 2024

FOREWORD

Mate-eeeeeeeee!!!!!!

Anyone who was devoted to the Uncle Doug Mulray era of Triple M in the 80's, would well remember the daily appearance of Frankie Vincent, bursting through the speakers, as the 'Inflatable Sports Guy' – his arrival signalled with a boisterous, Mate-eeee...after Mullos used a bike pump sound effect to blow him up! Frank was just another classic component to the crazy team that surrounded FM radio's greatest ever Sydney brekky host!

I've known Frank Vincent a long time. In fact, I first met him when I was still in a school uniform. As a cool jock at 2WL in Wollongong in the late 70's, Frank rocked along to my local high school to be a judge for the Miss Smiths' Hill contest. He can't even recall that moment (yeah – right), but our paths eventually crossed professionally in a newsroom 25 floors up in a tower in Bondi Junction.

Sport has always been what floats Frankie's boat. His passion often far exceeded his skill level, but that was just a mere hurdle. It's taken him to all corners of the world. It's propelled him into major sporting events that he only ever dreamed about covering. Over the years, I've been on the receiving end of random calls from Frank from mega-stadiums or airport lounges, with a cheeky "Sweetie-darling – you'll never believe where I am!"

Frank is a bloody funny bloke with the gift of the gab, the power of persuasion and the resilience of prize fighter. These traits continue to serve him well and drive all of us crazy as you know!

About to take one of Mulray's precious Jags for a spin.

In this book, Frank hopes the recollections bring back a burst of good times and memories that might be a little blurry thanks to a thousand beers or bourbons and other substances. But hey – that's rock'n'roll and truly, you really had to be there!

To your friend and mine, Frank has swapped being inflatable for being indefeasible. As the great Lionel Messi says, "You have to fight to reach your dream."

Much love,
Alison Drower

FM radio legends at the Ms. Left to right: Pete Armstrong, John Bell, me, Jono Coleman, Bob Gallagher, Doug Mulray, Ian Rogerson and Stuart Cranny.

CHAPTER 1

MAD, MERCURIAL UNCLE DOUG

On the 30th of March 2023 a legend of Australian radio signed-off for the final time. At the age of 71 Doug Mulray succumbed to liver cancer, but he had long since sealed his immortality with a legacy of laughter and unbridled joy for legions of listeners destined to never again tune-in to the likes of such a genius.

As a young radio announcer working on the good ship Mulray, commanded from the bridge of 2-Triple M's fabled Studio A, I simply could not have imagined the absolute privilege of working on a show that would catapult my career to new dizzying, heights. But I was lucky enough be one of the carriages on Mulray's runaway train – as it ran away with the ratings in a record setting streak of Sydney survey victories.

The airwaves had never been affronted with such raucous irreverence – and TV wasn't spared either. In September 1992 late media mogul Kerry Packer ordered the plug to be pulled on Doug's outrageous *Naughtiest Home Videos*.

"*Get that shit off air!*" the Channel Nine owner famously barked, leading Doug to later claim: "*I am the first man in Australian history to be pulled off by Kerry Packer.*" Maybe the visionary television king who saw the future with World Series Cricket also had a crystal ball for the infamous 21st century cancel culture that would almost certainly have had zero tolerance for the wicked wit of Mulray's mercurial mind!

At the height of his powers Mulray could have demolished any attempts of censorship by a self-appointed cognoscenti attempting to set the tone for the public sensibilities. From what I could tell there was just one rule on the Mulray show: *There are no rules!* The audacious declaration hit a bullseye in the heart of this young rebel, aching to swap my graveyard shift at Triple M for the skull and cross bones of Mulray's ensign.

The familiar taste of success at the Ms was always in the form of the best champagne, and like everybody else, I found these celebrations a hard habit to break!

Long before the internet a clear, starry night could deliver a strong signal from the transmitters of Sydney radio stations to country towns and regional cities beyond the Great Dividing Range. It was impossible to tune in through daylight hours but after dusk you could start to listen to the likes of 2SM, and one could at least pretend to be in Sydney. This vicarious indulgence is actually allowed by the setting of the sun. You see, radio waves naturally travel in straight lines, so it would be natural enough to assume the curvature of the earth would prevent radio stations from transmitting beyond 60 kilometres. That does apply to ground-based television transmissions. But a few radio stations, including 2SM, can take advantage of the short wave and AM bands to send their sound much further with startling clarity. Short wave can circle the planet, allowing AM stations to be heard for hundreds of miles at night when the sun's rays stop removing electrons from the atoms of the ionosphere. I always thought science could provide a perfectly simple explanation for these phenomena!

The above process allowed me to tune into 2SM from where I had cracked my first capital city gig in Canberra, and kept me acquainted with the styles of top-rating announcers at the top of their game, and right up to speed with the very latest music programming. And of course, I would make the most of my weekends away in Sydney to stay in touch by searching for the stronger daytime signals as I headed north up the Hume Highway.

My careful attention to the trends of the evolving Sydney radio market allowed me to track the emergence of a new player that would transform the industry as we had known it since that other great Italian Guglielmo Marconi invented wireless communication (before lending his name to my first Sydney soccer club, but that's a story for another chapter) The disrupter happened to share my initials. FM was a form of broadcasting using frequency modulation, and was invented 50 years before it finally took our industry by storm. American engineer Edwin Armstrong came up with FM in 1933 in his successful quest to provide a high fidelity signal over broadcast radio, more faithful to the sound of original recordings, and less prone to interference, static and the popping sounds that dogged the AM band.

But for various reasons, mainly associated with regulations and the limited availability of FM licences, this hi-fi version of radio didn't become ubiquitous until 1978, when the number of FM stations in the United States exceeded the total of AM broadcasters for the first time.

The wiser business heads of Australian broadcasting included former radio announcer Rod Muir. He was a rebel with a razor-sharp mercantile eye and had a clear vision of the future. By 1980 Muir had secured one of only two commercial FM licences available for the

The legend himself Doug Mulray in Triple M's Studio A, poached from 2 Double J before becoming Sydney's undisputed King of the Cornflakes.

Sydney market, and an icon of Australian radio was born – 2MMM.

Muir set about assembling a star-studded cast of announcers for his new venture, and in the stealthy tradition of Guy Fawkes, stashed enough 'gunpowder' into the basement of the Australian radio industry to blow its roof off! By the time the incumbent stations countered with their lame response of Stereo AM it was too late, and they suddenly had all the vulnerability of the timber-decked HMAS *Hood* in its one sided battle with the *Bismarck*.

2MMM first graced the airwaves on August 1980 2nd, 24 hours after the government owned 2JJJ joined the FM band. 2Day FM received the only other commercial licence, but 2MMM's rock format would prevail over its rival's easy listening schedule, while starting to make serious inroads on the incumbent AM rock'n'roll ruler 2SM.

Muir's masterstroke was to poach JJJ's Doug Mulray, who would go on to become Sydney's *King of the Cornflakes* – an irreverent renegade who would rewrite the manual on breakfast radio entertainment. Muir's approach to conquering the Sydney market was straight out of the playbook used by Kerry Packer just a few years earlier when the mogul took on the cricket establishment to set-up World Series Cricket by signing-up the sport's biggest names. Mulray was the Doug Walters of radio, an already popular larrikin bound to command a strong following. It didn't matter what microphone he sat behind. Mulray could make people laugh just by reading out the names from the telephone book. He was funnier than a fart in a bath, a natural born comic with the sharpness of his rock 'n roll knowledge matched only by the knife that was his tongue.

As *60 Minutes* reported in 1989: *"He's the kind of DJ who makes*

Dave Gibson, aka Roland Roll-a-door, with my first wife Victoria at a Triple M party I hosted in Balmain.

it hard to digest your breakfast. He's sharp. He's vulgar, and he's profoundly funny. The most original act on radio. Uncle Doug to his audience, Mullos to his friends, Mulray is the kind of breakfast announcer who never ceases to daze and amaze."

With Triple M promotions coordinator Stacey Boyd.

Sydney radio had known nothing like *The Doug Mulray Show*. Until then the early morning humour had been limited to 2UE's long standing ratings guru Garry O'Callaghan and a fictional bird known as Sammy Sparrow – the announcer's foil for a string of endearing Dad jokes. If Garry was a father figure, Doug was definitely the Mad Uncle! A mad *rich* uncle!

Oscar Wilde always insisted the difference between *eccentricity, and madness* was *money*. Doug wasn't rich enough to qualify for the former – at least not yet. Doug would adopt the *Uncle Doug* handle and ended-up becoming the highest paid announcer in the history of Australian radio but ultimately his brand of genius was priceless. Nobody had dared to push the boundaries of censorship with such gay abandon before a massive audience, but Doug danced along that line every morning from the moment he opened his mic to the very end when he'd sign off with the wicked double entendre "I'll cop you later" which was always designed to mean "I'll copulater." If his listeners weren't spitting out their coffee they were running off the road as Doug and his madcap crew turned the 6am–9am shift into a daily comedy feast to provide the biggest laughs on radio since Peter Sellers, Spike Milligan and Harry Secombe transfixed millions of listeners with The Goons 30 years earlier.

As if Doug weren't funny enough, his act soared to new hysterical heights with the injections of his sidekick Dave Gibson, the unsung hero in the story of Triple M's stunning success. Dave was a master of oral disguises, appearing on the Mulray show in the form of several characters including Roland Roll-a-door from *Roland Roll-a-door's Roll-a-doors.*

"You're not after a plug by any chance?" Doug would always ask when Roland phoned in with his free advice.

There was the day when Roland called on the occasion of the Berlin wall's collapse, suggesting one of his trusty products could be installed should the East Germans rethink their decision to join the free democratic world. You'll be hearing from Roland again in this book. 34 years later he's still not short of a word and he insisted on having the last one on my life story!

Then there was Jack Africa, the parody of the lunatic listener who often phoned me and every other midnight to dawn announcer with their kooky conspiracy theories.

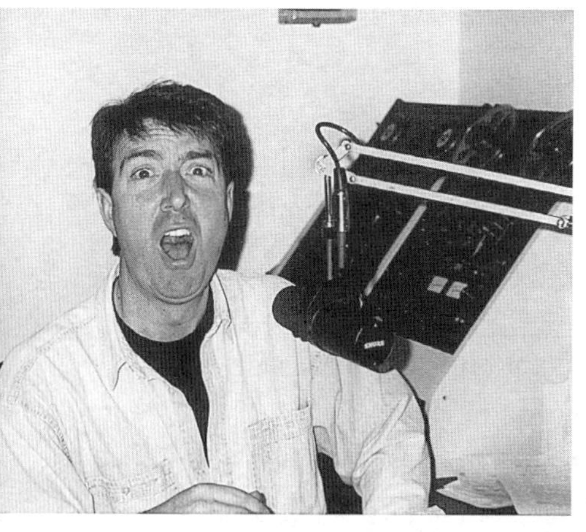

"Ron E! It's not working!" My great friend and inspiration from Triple M, afternoon announcer Ron E Sparx.

"Hey Mullos," Jack would say. "I can't stop knitting, Mullos."

"You can't stop knitting, Jack? Why would that be, Jack?" Doug would ask.

"I snorted Nanna's ashes, Mullos!"

Gibson modelled Jack Africa's voice on the traffic

reporter Warwick Rankin, or *Warwick the Barking Traffic Girl*, as Doug called him. Warwick was a legend of Sydney radio and television. The former Commander Strongarm of the Channel TEN kids' show fame, joined Triple M in his late 50s, ostensibly to guide listeners through the chaos of the city's peak hour motoring, made even worse as drivers struggled to stay in control of their cars as Doug challenged their composure at the wheel with his gut busting gags. Warwick's off mic antics were even wilder than his on-air shenanigans – which included using his authentic bark to spook police sniffer dogs searching for any bombs that may have been planted in the studios ahead of a visit by then Prime Minister Bob Hawke. The dogs had a much better chance of finding leafy green substances at Triple M than any explosive device, so I sensed that's exactly why Warwick was attempting to throw them off the scent. One of Warwick's favourite stunts involved the insertion of goldfish into the office water coolers. One morning staff arrived to find every chair in the Triple M offices had been locked in the production studio, years before it became ergonomically fashionable to stand at your desk. And somehow the newsroom plants managed to include

Here I am with Triple M promos staffer Sue Ellen Stock, nodding very politely to Calabrian ancestors, and she did a great job as my gangster dame.

With my good mate Jim Beam, preparing for my midnight to dawn shift!

one shrub with incredible disappearing leaves. Warwick also loved the expression 'up the stick' referring to a radio station's transmitter. "All that matters Mullos is what goes *up the stick!*" That was his signature saying.

When Doug was recently inducted into the Commercial Radio Hall of Fame he was very keen to honour the integral role played in his success by the crazy cast that became known as the *Mulray Bunch.*

"Remarkable really, that we can have fantastic recognition of 15 years of partying really," he said in his acceptance speech.

"I had fun. It was a near death experience, but I survived. And we were able to share studios at Triple M in those days with some extraordinary talented people". He singled out Dave Gibson for special praise.

"David Gibson – who never appeared as David Gibson – but in

Reviving the MC skills I developed as a teenager as the Master of Ceremonies at the wedding of Triple M Colleague Rob Duckworth, pulling-off my Paul Keating doppelgänger!

many different forms many different guises, which was fair because he had multiple personality disorder. It seemed a perfectly reasonable way of treating him!

Then he recalled another sublime story about Warwick, he described as "quite the strangest man I ever knew."

"Stories to tell about him are many and various including the time we had a tiger in the studio to promote the Sunnyboys album *Wildcat* – I think it was.

"They brought a 700 pound Bengal tiger into the studio and there's a 90-year-old man holding him with a piece of chain.

"The tiger's not happy, gets out of the lift on the 25th floor of Triple M and shits everywhere and then he's rolling it just to get his

With Jono Coleman, Pete Armstrong, John Bell (sitting) and Triple M Drive Announcer Rob Duckworth.

smell into the carpet so he felt more comfortable.

"When we were in the studio – terrified but carrying on because the show must go on – Warwick decided to stick his head in the door and bark at the tiger.

"In fact, I nearly joined the tiger and shat on the floor and rolled in it myself!"

As Doug remarked at the time it was "a big cat that smells just like a little pussy, really."

Doug also paid tribute to his legendary writer Ken Sterling, employed personally by Doug after Rod Muir refused to hire him from where they had first collaborated on JJJ.

"Rod said: 'I'm not employing any fucking writers.' So, I took the money that I negotiated and gave Ken half because I believed that what we could do was create production values again the way radio had been in its halcyon days."

He praised Muir for introducing FM to Australia, after Dougie had become his brother in law via marriage to his boss's sister Lizzie.

"If it wasn't for Rod, we'd never have had the medium, Triple M came into being and well we were owned by one man and we were unique...a go-to environment.

"Everybody who worked in radio in Australia wanted to work there. And I was lucky enough to be one of them.

"It'd be dumb for me to receive this award without acknowledging those people and I think that too often when my success is discussed they're overlooked, and I really couldn't accept this award without including them in my thank you. We fashioned coterie of learners and gradually built the audience from 2.6 up to the high teens and brought a lot of people a lot of joy but mostly us and it was a thrill to be there."

The owners were thrilled too. Advertisers flocked to the Ms as Mulray stamped himself as the hottest property on the airwaves.

The secret of Doug's success in making people laugh was due to his innate understanding of the audience, and as he told *60 Minutes* in 1989, he could often be far from amusing when he succumbed to the inevitable darker, private side of the public clown.

"I get very black moods," he told the interviewer.

"And it's very hard to dig myself out of the emotional mire in which I find myself...what I think are the very ugly circumstances in which we live. So, I'm talking about empathizing with the miserable creatures on the face of the earth... and that I do little or nothing for them apart from make them laugh occasionally and making fart jokes isn't exactly a great contribution to culture."

He was sheepish about his earnings in the interview, leaning to the need for privacy but completely candid about his copious consumption of booze.

"I drink too much," he confessed.

"In fact, I've just been told that I have far too many enzymes in my liver for the destruction of alcohol.

"A bottle of wine is – well...probably too much. That's during the show. I get off air at nine and have a bourbon and coke, and a couple of drinks for lunch. And then go home and have some real drinks with dinner....so relaxing but it certainly hasn't helped the waistline."

But for as long the Triple M *bottom line* was looking so healthy nobody was going to complain about Doug's rockstar indulgences, which he recalled with what you may well call 'smoky eyed' sentiment in his Hall of Fame acceptance speech.

"We went into the newsroom, and somebody had just arrived from the north coast with a kilogram of purple heads. And they were measuring them out in bags to different staff members who are queuing up to buy their little dilly. Quite extraordinary. Really, I thought this *is* the station for me, and I thought the Jays had been cool!"

Its owner Rod Muir was a born winner. One of his more famous quotes was delivered whenever he cracked the bubbly to celebrate yet another ratings win. "Champagne! Jeez success is easy to cop!" And then there was his famous: "Number one is all that matters. Everything else is bullshit." Muir's bullish mantra was completely consistent with the theme of Channel Nine's ratings conquering CEO Sam Chisolm. "Winners have parties. Losers have meetings."

You can imagine how cool it was for me to take a phone call from my old 2CC college Keith Williams to advise that I should send a tape to the 2 Triple M program director Trevor Smith. My heart was in my mouth. This was the moment I had dreamt about for so long. I was on the cusp of realising my loftiest ambition, and like that Bengal Tiger my bowels were loosening, my throat was tightening, adrenaline was pumping and heart just thumping. I sent in my reel in record speed and the job was mine – back on the graveyard shift but as far as 'radio cemeteries' go this was headstone heaven! With Triple M flying high on the wings of the Doctor Dan logo with Mulray in the pilot's seat I was suddenly soaring to heights I would once only dare to imagine. My first thought was: *"Shit. Am I up to this?"* I was riddled with doubt one minute and just as quickly puffed with the pride of knowing I had won radio's equivalent of a fluffy green Australian cricket cap. I was on the team. The number one team in the land. I might have been 'batting down the order' but I was in the 'first eleven' and looking for superlatives that would do my feelings more justice than simply 'ecstatic.' Any sneaking feeling of imposter syndrome evaporated when my first Triple M First Christmas Party featured an impromptu unplugged performance from the legendary Richard Clapton.

My old mate Duckworth had already been hired for the afternoon shift, and I was also reunited with my Wollongong buddy from 2 Double 0 Dave Carlson, who would pull the shift from 10pm to 2am, when I would slip into the chair for the best view of the Sydney night sky, from the seventh heaven on level 25 of the Bondi Junction office building that became the fabled home of Sydney's new radio ratings juggernaut.

It was quite daunting to suddenly find myself in the company of so many talented announcers, but foolishly I almost blew my golden chance just weeks after starting. Thinking I was getting into the wild Triple M spirit of things I rolled this fat joint and almost drove my career over a cliff. This weed was industrial strength, direct from Jamaica, and hit me for six. Thinking it would relax me the number had the opposite effect, and soon I was a sweating ball of paranoia, and slurring my delivery. I was just extremely lucky that the audience in the wee small hours was commensurately tiny, and I would somehow escape the verge of career suicide. The only rule about smoking at Tripe M: "yeah you can smoke but don't fuck-up" and here I was fucking-up big time.

Shortly after a young lady cornered me and asked where the coke was: "This is triple M right? So, where's all the cocaine?"

It was a great time to be joining Australia's leading rock station as a long list of Aussie bands dominated the charts, Midnight Oil, Rose Tattoo, The Angels, Australian Crawl, INXS, The Divinyls, Cold Chisel, Split Enz, Dragon, The Church, Flowers, Mental As Anything and Nick Cave were all hitting their straps as their popularity only grew on the back of Triple M's assurance of high rotation for their chart busting hits.

The brightest star of them all Michael Hutchence was speeding towards his legendary Rock God status as the world began to discover the talents of a charismatic front man often compared with Jim Morrison. It was such a high to have the likes of INXS blasting out of the studio speakers, and soon I was inviting friends to join me in the dead of the night for an impromptu party high above the sleeping metropolis. Luckily those slumbering away included the station executives, who never woke up to the liberties I was taking with a long list of my own very special station guests!

Leaving Canberra had the sensation of lifting the lid of a leaden coffin, and I didn't waste any time embracing the lively Sydney lifestyle. Life was suddenly dynamic and three dimensional again, and at the tender age of 25 I was ready to take a deep dive into the party pool, becoming a regular at the Kardomah Café, where I was lucky enough once to witness Mick Jagger in an impromptu performance witnessed by a select few. It was amazing to see this rusted-on legend strut his stuff in front of only 100 people. I've never seen such a larger-than-life figure on such a small stage. I didn't meet Jagger, but it was still a very special privilege to see him live in this very intimate setting.

The Jagger 'pop-up' gig gave me a sharp sense of the 'big time' I had been craving for so long, and as Kings Cross roared with its trademark racket life was suddenly much more colourful than the Orwellian stillness of the sleepy national capital.

CHAPTER 2

THE INFLATABLE BLACK RAT

If you're starting to gather Triple M in the 1980s was just one big party your instincts are not letting you down.

With one survey victory after another only the music and the laughs flowed faster than the champagne as the format of classic rock, comedy and general irreverence built-up an army of loyal listeners.

Now the Ms wasn't exactly known as a news station but its ratings bonanza still attracted a raft of quality journos who would eventually leave to pursue the more serious side of their craft.

There was the super cool Terry Mabb, the delightful Margaret Bates, the debonair News Director and mad Manly supporter David 'Maroon and White', Alison Drower, Deanne Bishop and my good mate Adam Walters. Margaret and Adam both left to pursue TV careers, following Allison who became the host of MTV and Deanne ended-up heading back to her native Perth.

Then there was me. After convincing Mullos he needed a sports reporter, I came off the graveyard shift and stepped onto the roller-coaster of weekday breakfast in what would become a slingshot for my career.

Warwick Rankin had already christened me The Black Rat. The pale-faced Dave Carlson was known as the White Mouse, and when I once rocked up to the pub with him Warwick said: "Here they are – the White Mouse and The Black Rat." And it stuck.

But Mullos had other ideas. He was single-minded about ditching the anglicisation of my handle and insisted my birth name be resurrected for his own wicked purposes of course! To the delight of my parents and the wider Italian community of Sydney's west *Francesco Vincenzo Movizio* was making his radio debut. Mulray never missed an opportunity to mention my name. He would only have to back announce a song from the super group Foreigner, and he'd be at it again. "And that was Foreigner – and that reminds us: next up we have Francesco Vincenzo Movizio with a look at today's sport." And on it went. But the natural born shit stirrer Dougie wasn't finished with my 'rebranding' just yet. He then gave me the title of the *Inflatable Sports Reporter*. David Gibson would provide the sound effects for my 'inflation' and with a loud pop at the end of his mock pumping effect to complete this superb theatre of the mind I'd spring to life with what became my signature greeting to all. "Mate-eeeeeeeee!!!!!!" Doug was making a habit of targeting me, but I always laughed along, even if his comments bordered on the

Triple News Director and breakfast reader David 'Maroon and' White always denied ironing his pyjamas … an allegation by the madcap Mulray that never stuck.

The Black Rat in drag! Australian netballers Keelie Devrey and Clarissa Dalwood measure me up for a try out before I had a chance to shave down.

sort of cruelty that would be barely tolerated in the modern workplace. Even my physical features were fair game. After I broke my rather prominent nose in a car accident once Doug reported to the listeners that I was hospitalised in a critical condition with injuries to '90 per cent' of my body! Now that was harsh! Talk about insult to injury.....

Like former jock David White I was finding news a great way to be included on the on-air team of what became the fabled music station success story of the late 20th century as the FM band continued to conquer the world.

Now to say I was a square peg in a round hole may have been a slight understatement. News wasn't exactly my bag or ever coveted but I grew to love the immediacy of breaking stories and, as always, there was no shortage of colourful yarns from the fields of competitive play at a time when State of Origin Rugby League was cementing its legendary status.

Now these were wild days.

I remember the 'straighty 180' journos in the newsroom were quite shocked by the hijinks in those spectacular wood panelled studios with their sweeping views over Sydney Harbour.

I was still getting my head around headlines and deadlines – and as any old journo will tell you – the news waits for no man – not even me.

A young Adam Walters, now a veteran television reporter, had the tough task of arriving at 4am and tearing-up the reams of wire service copy paper strewn all over the newsroom floor. Walters was no 'rip and read' man.

All this copy had to be sorted into baskets and then the better stories were rewritten in the tongue in cheek Triple M style.

For example, when the super suave Andrew Peacock rolled John Howard for the coalition leadership in 1989 our bulletin would report that "the coalition leadership has woken this morning without its spectacles and bushy eyebrows – and is suddenly sporting a suntan." Try getting away with that on the ABC. It was all written to suit the style of the stylish David Whyte in the Doug Mulray show. Mullos rarely left Whitey alone either. David was known for his sartorial splendour and reliably immaculate presentation – the only person in the daily habit of wearing a snappy suit and tie on level 25. If he ever ran late Mullos would explain to listeners that Whitey was "still at home – ironing his pyjamas."

Walters would also read the news between nine and midday on the Stuart Cranny show.

AW would make just as much mischief with my copy for the 7am sport report, loading me up with dreadful puns for which I had to take ultimate responsibility and he chuckled like a demented Mutley as I broadcast them to an audience forced to have a little *too much* corn with their flakes.

But one morning he was in no way prepared to take my sudden absence lightly just minutes before I was due on air.

Walters finally found me in the fire escape – lighting my own

– at the end of a tightly rolled little breakfast number. And no – I wasn't smoking Weetbix!

But hey! This was Triple M! I managed to get the report to air, and a bemused breakfast editor just shook his head as if to say: "*Who am I? And what the fuck am I doing here??!!*"

Walters went on to become a sports reporter himself in an ill-fated move to Channel 10 just as the Network was preparing for mass redundancies – that included him a mere three months after leaving us. He bounced back quickly, resuming a newspaper career with a gig at *The Daily Telegraph* before joining Seven and Nine 10 years later as a crime reporter.

He was one of three journos to join us from the hits and memories station 2WS, following Deanne Bishop and Alison Drower.

The shock to their system must have been heavy when they arrived at the Ms to find the water coolers turned into aquariums, a destroyed Doug Mulray snoring on the reception lounge under a blanket of empty champagne bottles and every single chair in the joint hidden by the habitual prankster Warwick 'The Barking Traffic Girl' Rankin.

I was revelling in my newfound 'fame' and mixing it with Sydney's glitterati in the swankest haunts of the rich and famous, including a magnet for the superstars of world showbiz known as The Sebel Town House. I walked in there one night looking for my old buddy and popular rock jock Paul Holmes. As I waited to meet him, I found myself at the bar running into the state promotions manager of EMI records David Baxter. He introduced me to an English fellow with an educated accent. "Frank, I'd like you to meet Andrew." Now this bloke had a very familiar face, which is just as well because I missed his name in the introduction. Andrew turned out to be Andrew of the Lloyd Webber fame! It was my honour to buy him a glass of chardonnay and chat with a living legend. If he was being polite by managing to chuckle at my suggestion that his next musical should be *Dogs*, I certainly would have forgiven the great man for any acting performance of his own!

Meeting the father of the modern musical theatre was just one of many occasions on which this boy from suburban Fairfield was found to be pinching himself. The job at Triple M had catapulted me into another galaxy – my universe was now full of stars, some of the biggest and brightest of the 1980s. There was never a moment when I took this amazing job for granted, and with it came the keys to the city. Triple M was Sydney's uber cool radio station and the biggest names in Australian and international showbiz were queuing up to bang on the studio door.

I was busy building my own relatively humble profile and making the most of any chances that came my way to bathe in the glow of the megastars who filed in and out of the Ms almost every day. The stars loved the atmosphere of the studios. INXS and Richard Clapton were our biggest home-grown fans. Clapton was mad about the Ms. Michael Hutchence and the boys would make regular random appearances on the Mulray show – and Doug would always be welcoming, on the strict condition their publicist would send them in with a bottle of French champagne! As if the bubbly were ever needed after most of the breakfast crew had already been on the high of sucking on a fat joint habitually rolled and shared before every show. It was a ritual not even the Federal Police sniffer dogs could interrupt. Mulray always amazed me with his incredible composure in spite of the gang's conspicuous consumption. He was as sharp as a tack, but I couldn't say the same for myself. It was a real challenge to be straight by 7.40am for my daily sports spot – and maybe that's why the boys thought I was in need of 'inflation.' Every day they set a cracking pace and it was a struggle for any mere mortal to keep up. It was hard enough to keep track of my various names. To the completely incidental delight of my proud parents, oblivious to the actual piss take, Doug persisted with the Francesco Vincenzo Movizio intro, Whitey stuck with *The Black Rat* and poor old *Frank Vincent* – my actual stage name – was barely getting a run! But I wasn't complaining. Work was suddenly a paid hobby, or even better than that, I felt like a professional party goer, actually collecting a pay cheque every week for laughs, experiences and memories no amount of money could ever buy. And I was still in my late 20s – a veritable lad in the grand arc of time but certainly a lot wiser to the world than the gormless son of immigrant parents setting out to build a new life on the sunburnt streets of Sydney's west – where my story began.

CHAPTER 3

THE WILD WEST

When my grandparents fled the ravages of war-torn Italy, they thought they were headed for the lucky country, among thousands of Italians seeking to build a new life down under. My parents were still young children as the Movizio family set sail towards the bottom of the earth, still largely unscathed from the horrors of global conflict.

Australia was soon delivering on its reputation as the promised land as our family settled in the apparently peaceful semi-rural districts of Sydney's outer west.

A large part of the family's planning for the future involved the arranged marriage of my parents. There was the narrowest margin for romance in these challenging, pragmatic times – and my mother and father had little say in the decision to make them husband and wife. There were no eyes meeting across the room in a whimsical discovery of true love, just a carefully managed union of two families seeking to establish security in numbers.

By the time I arrived on the scene at Fairfield Hospital on April 27th 1957 my father was working as a motor mechanic and

The age of innocence. In my backyard at Fairfield, oblivious to the horrors awaiting me at the local Schools.

Dressed for the "wild west" — if only my Sherriff's badge was of any use!

the latest generation of the Movizio family was making a solid start a world away from the ancestorial farms in the southern Italian region of Calabria.

But in complete defiance of our family's hopes for a happy, peaceful life this gormless infant could hardly have suspected he was arriving in a world of bigotry and racism, ready to deliver a childhood that was anxious at best and miserable most of the time.

I'm not suggesting for a second that I was born at the 'back of the grid'. My parents worked hard to deliver a relatively comfortable life, and there was no greater comfort than their unwavering love and care for me and my older brother. We lived in a small but well-appointed home in the then new suburb of Fairfield. A large tree in a nearby park dominates my memory as a pre-schooler, and my passion for climbing it would go on to become a metaphor for the heights I was determined to scale later in my life.

But in the meantime, the Catholic Education system would do its best to make life in Fairfield a seemingly endless marathon of misery, starting with my enrolment at Our Lady of the Rosary Primary School. This was the setting for the first of many beatings I'd receive from the clergy claiming to be proxies for the late, great Jesus Christ. In my mind, according to my rudimentary understanding of Catholic theology, the so called divinity of the nuns and brothers was dubious enough to strongly suggest they were in fact the devil in black disguise. To say they were cruel almost borders on understatement. Their vile tempers and violent assaults of terrified and defenceless young children plunged way below any definition of acceptable 'discipline' to bear closer resemblance to the sadism one might imagine in hell itself.

I've often been bemused by the expression 'lapsed' catholic. '*Collapsed*' is much more like it. Such was the weight of the unrelenting terror inflicted upon the weakest of victims.

My first flogging came as an eight-year-old. My sin? Writing down the letter 'R'. That's R as in *radical, retribution, racism, ruthless* and *ruler*....as in the weapon chosen to punish my constant struggle to shape it with a pencil.

My parents reacted to spectacle of my red raw knuckles with the horror you'd expect from any loving mother and father entrusting the church with the day-to-day care of a young child.

Like millions of Catholics these days I have sat back and watched the church brought to account for the multi-generational sexual abuse of children and I have cheered-on and felt deeply for every victim as their harrowing tales were presented to a Royal Commission that exposed this institution for the decades of evil that has crushed so many lives.

But for all the appalling behaviour of the depraved deviants who violated young children sexually there are many more who also inflicted thoroughly unjustified physical harm on students in a brutal court of summary 'justice.' The smallest of misdemeanours would be met with an instant, savage response. Just gazing out of a classroom window for a moment's contemplation of a happier world, a harmless but necessary daydream, could be met with a sudden lash from a cane or a short stiff strap that resembled – and actually felt like – a length of timber.

The nun's outrageous conduct at *Our Lady of the Rosary* was just a sinister sign of much worse to come at the local Catholic boys high school.

Patrician Brothers Fairfield liked to project its image from the school's success as a breeding ground for champion Rugby League players. But the reality of day-to-day life for most students amounted to a bitter existence of fear and loathing.The abuse was coming from every direction in the Catholic education system, dished-out by brothers struggling and mostly failing to manage the malevolent manifestations of their wholly unnatural enforced celibacy. This suppression of their God-given testosterone would create a production line of monsters with tortured souls far darker than their black uniforms. The behaviour was brutal and brazen. The brothers had their favourites, usually those wretched students

Blackboard jungle — this collection of smiles tells a million lies about the reality of our misery at Patrician Brothers. That's me right above the sign.

enlisted to provide the evil brutes with sexual relief. These assaults didn't always take place in the dim, chalk-dusted dungeons of locked storerooms, but in the broad daylight of an actual classroom. There was one who would position his target on a desk at the back of the room, and this Godforsaken child was tasked with masturbating the teacher's penis as his classmates were forced to listen to the atrocity, not daring to look around for the fear of a much worse 'flogging'.

I hated school – every minute of it. It wasn't just the staff to be feared. Other students had their own role to play in the ongoing intimidation. In fact, the brothers often enlisted class captains as *deputy demons* in their absence, and they'd report any student considered worthy of a lashing. If a teacher was running late for class the captain would stand at the front with a piece of chalk as his weapon, ready to adorn the blackboard with the initials of anyone he didn't like. The teacher would then inspect the list on arrival and order the accused to the front of the class for their mandatory caning. One didn't have to be singled-out to be traumatised while witnessing the beatings of students you knew to be completely innocent.

But alas, I was among the victims, and was even strapped once for the sin of sweeping the classroom floor! This was at a time when society was a long

With my mother Mary, father Vince and brother Sam.

way off from opening its blind eyes to child abuse. The rationale for this contrived ignorance was sinister itself – and went like this: "*If you didn't see it – it didn't happen*". The Catholic Church, as we now know, was complicit in concealing these awful crimes, and I can't recall seeing a single police officer walk through the gates of Patrician Brothers to start examining the scenes of so many daily atrocities.

It's not as if there were any respite offered by the sunburnt tundra of Fairfield's suburban streets. The irony of the suburb's name was never lost on me. There was nothing fair about this far-flung field on the edge of the Sydney metropolis. It should have been called *Mine Field* – a booby trapped maze of menacing no-go zones, and none more dangerous than the platforms of the local railway stations.

Fairfield Station was a place I tried to avoid at all costs, populated by racist thugs ready to torment and bash anyone of ethnic descent. As punishment for his Italian heritage one of my uncles had a rock thrown squarely at his face. The missile smashed his teeth and caused lifelong complications for his dental health. His prolonged ordeal alone has kept these awful memories of a racist Australia in sharp focus to this day, and it's hard to forgive let alone forget. The streets, swimming pool and railway stations were meant to be centres of civic convenience and comfort but they were no place for the victims of vicious racism, and I was in the their ranks, relying on my own wits and an unlikely Praetorian Guard of young men from the nearby suburbs of Mt Pritchard, Rooty Hill and Liverpool. They seemed to relish the opportunity to flog the Fairfield thugs in the ostensible interest of protecting their targets. We might have been their worthy excuse for belting the Fairfield lads, but I was never going to complain for as long as they effectively became my incidental body guards.

My father was an accomplished amateur boxer and I often lamented the lack of any genetic inheritance in the fighting department. God knows I felt like punching back but despite his skills on the canvas Dad was a pacifist and the only things he was ever beating were the dents of panels in his car body repair shop. He was known as a gentle man and was very popular in the community.

So as my parents encouraged me to turn the other cheek I resorted to humour as my first and last lines of defence. From my early high school years, I could make people laugh and my one liners and joke telling seemed to provide a certain level of protection. As my audience grew so did my confidence and by the age of 14 I was handling my first microphone as the Master of Ceremonies at a local eisteddfod. I had no way of predicting then that a microphone would become such an intrinsic part of my adult life but at the time I was more than happy to acquaint myself with the skill of saying the right thing at the right time. Soon I was hosting functions staged by local families and friends. School, meanwhile, was as unfulfiling as ever – a 13-year sentence for a crime I never committed, other than the transgression of being born a Catholic. But somehow, I rose above the fear, and counted down the days, one by one crossing them off the 'cell wall' and amusing myself in the meantime. The absence of girls didn't make life any easier. The public-school boys were so relaxed and comfortable in the company of the fillies and I would envy the ease and confidence with which they would move among them. I would have to wait until the end of year 12 before contemplating such a luxury.

There was nothing those great lads from the neighbouring suburbs could do to protect me from the thuggery inside the imposing gates and walls the Patrician Brothers, but by the age of 17 I was having the last of my bashings, smashed in the face by a brother in Year 11. As boys were becoming men, perfectly capable of fighting back, the brothers narrowed their target range to the smaller students among us – and by year 12, when we started to enter the adult world, most of our tormentors were backing-off as the common law loomed as an ominous replacement of the school's punitive and arbitrary rules.

In my final school years I maintained a determination to never darken the doorstep of any educational institution again, and while I was more than competent in the areas of English, History, Geography and Economics I was in no way prepared to even begin contemplating university study. I was done. Any aspirations for tertiary pursuits had been literally flogged out of me, and the very idea of being locked-up in a lecture theatre was a sickening, suffocating scenario as the wider world beckoned. The sniff of that promise started arriving years earlier via a sea breeze on family trips to Bronte Beach in Sydney's eastern suburbs. That was a major expedition back in the day. I can still picture the maps being unfurled on the kitchen table as my father and uncles plotted our journey for the big day out. It'd stand on the golden sands of Bronte and stare towards the clean, crisp line of the horizon and wonder what exactly lay beyond it – for me.

It's not that I wasn't

My first meeting with Santa – decades before we reunited on his turf in Lapland.

ambitious by ruling out university. Far from it. My modest success as an amateur DJ, MC and public speaker had me dreaming about a career as a professional broadcaster. I was a huge fan of radio, and particularly fond of then famous 2UW announcer Ward Pally Austin. I followed his career closely and almost idolised him. He was one of radio's original hellraisers, and it seemed barely a day would pass without a headline about his wild and whacky life off the air. He was once raided by the police for unlicensed firearm possession after they seized his Remington revolver. Then there was his notorious nightclub brawl with comedian Joe Martin, and in 1970 the infamy of allegedly racist remarks to Sammy Davis Jr. He was then sacked by 2UW and moved to New Zealand before applying for permanent United States residency to take up a gig at KXIV in Phoenix Arizona. By 1975 he was forgiven for his earlier sins and reemployed by 2UW. Although the Coogee born and raised Austin was best known as *'Pally'*, his other nicknames included *'Baby'*, *'White Knight'*, *'Confederate Cowboy'* and *'Peter Pan of the Airwaves.'* Love or loathe him – there could be no argument about his colour as a dominant character on the Sydney airwaves, and he hooked me with his famous catchphrases such as *"a rickapoodie and a fandooglie"*, *"too much for the human unit"* and *"anytime you're ready, Pally."*

This guy was larger than life and my distant admiration became inspiration. I'd follow Ward's glamourous life via the social pages of the newspapers and pictured myself sharing the same 'front row seats' of life, far removed from what I then saw as the anonymous obscurity of western suburban Sydney. Defying the expectations of my family to 'get a real job' in law, architecture or heaven forbid – medicine – I had decided radio would be my highway out of what I saw as the mediocrity I seemed destined to tolerate without any lofty ambitions.

This dream coincided with the magnificent freedom provided by a driver's licence, and a panel van gifted by my father to make sure I'd stay off the motorcycles I was eyeing-off at the time. Soon I was meeting friends at the Sea Breeze Hotel and finally acquainting myself with the girls who had been so elusive and mysterious in those wretched years of incarceration at the boys' school.

I was very proud of my 'shaggin' wagon' as panel vans were known at the time, complete with its mural on the back gate, hand painted by one of Dad's workers at the panel beating shop. My vehicle became a strong symbol of the freedom I had craved for so long, and the independence I needed to shape the early days of my career as a disc jockey. It was perfect for transporting the turntables, records and speakers I was using to entertain the guests of weddings and other local functions with a dance floor. It was 1975, and I took great delight in sampling new songs in what turned out to be a golden era for popular music. There was no greater thrill than introducing a hitherto unheard track, well before it was even played on radio. I would trawl record shops for hours on end looking for such gems, and then there was the immense satisfaction of witnessing the rush to the dance floor when it played publicly for the very first time. All the while my confidence was growing in communicating with an audience, and my roving DJ act would turn out to be a perfect training ground for the career of my dreams. I couldn't have been sure where this journey was going to end, but I was dead certain of being on the right track towards a bigger, better and brighter life. If anything was to be said for the despair of my school years it would be the propulsion it provided towards heights, I may never have imagined had life had been a more dignified, peaceful affair.

Maybe if most of my time at school had actually been focused on study instead of day-to-day self-preservation, I could have eventually distinguished myself academically and beyond with a prestigious, well paid profession – more in line with maternal and paternal hopes. I still wanted to do Mum, Dad and the extended family proud – but I was prioritising the expectations I had of *myself.* I can understand why such a path would have been seen as unconventional, and even treacherous given the rarity of broadcasting jobs on offer and the even slimmer chances of rising to the very top in such a competitive industry. Aspiring actors share the same trepidation, before many of them earn a crust with more voice over work for commercials than any consistently well-paid performing roles on stage and screen. But I was single-minded – not to merely to prove the doubters wrong – but to prove myself *right*. It can sound corny to say one has had *a calling* – but I did every day, simply by tuning into 2UW. I could literally hear the *sound of success* from the voices of the station's star-studded line-up, that included a young Donnie Sutherland.

In The Patrician Brothers library — a refuge of sorts.

By sheer coincidence Donnie was a family friend, and he was fast establishing himself as a major Sydney media identity. In 1975 he had just turned 30 and was also launching his television career as presenter of Channel 7's pop music show *Sound Unlimited.* He was on the verge of becoming a household name, appearing every Saturday morning as seriously stiff competition to Molly Meldrum on the ABC's iconic *Countdown.*

Sound Unlimited was later shortened to *Sounds*, and initially broadcast to a Sydney audience before its popularity ensured a nationwide audience ahead of an amazing 16-year run featuring live performances from Aussie rock legends including Sherbet, John Paul Young, Jon English and Marcia Hines.

Donnie went on to host ratings blockbuster with a TV special on the *Greatest Hits of Olivia Newtown-John*, by then an international megastar thanks the global success of *Grease*.

From 1982 Donnie hosted a late-night music and chat show *After Dark*, and to know him in his radio days was more than an honour, but a privilege in convincing myself that such heights of success were not so impossible after all. So, by now, 2UW was becoming integral to my motivation for cracking the big time. And as you're about to read in the next chapter – Australia's best known hard rock act was about to play its own special role in turbo charging my career.

CHAPTER 4

THUNDERSTRUCK

As you may well have already gathered, I'm not known for being short of a word or two, but they truly fail me when trying to describe the sense of freedom I experienced after I walked out of the Patrician Brothers gates for the last time. The leaving certificate results didn't have to arrive for me to know I had already graduated from university – the fabled university of 'hard knocks', but there was nothing figurative about my alma mater. The hard knocks had been delivered by actual physical beatings – metered out by a sinister cohort of low-ranking Catholic clergy, symbolising anything but the Christian ideal of love, peace and compassion.

But any time of painful reflection was quickly replaced by the anticipation of shaping my own future in the fashion I had imagined so often on the marathon countdown towards genuine liberation. I was about to become my own best example of positive projection, and suddenly I was seeing way beyond that distant Bronte horizon which had been so hypnotically promising in my earlier years.

There was much more than the wheels of my panel van spinning furiously to speed me towards making dreams a reality – the turntables of my DJ decks were even more crucial as I was promoted from family and local community functions to service clubs and other venues combining a disco with live music. These were the glory days of the Australian music scene, and our artists were soon rivalling sporting heroes for prominence on the world stage. Many had launched their careers on *Bandstand*, mimicking the trajectory of new talent uncovered by Britain's *Top of the Pops*.

With family friend and mentor Donnie Sutherland, already a star in his right on radio and television. He was a great inspiration.

Then *Countdown* came along to replace *Bandstand* as the launch pad for stellar careers.

It was 1976 and the charts were dominated by ABBA's *Fernando*, rivalled only by the ongoing sales of Queen's October 1975 mega hit *Bohemian Rhapsody* as the biggest selling single of the year.

Sitting in the number four position was Australia's very own Sherbet with their smash hit *Howzat*. Daryl Braithwaite and the boys were joined by the lads from the Ted Mulry Gang, Marcia Hines and John Paul Young as the other home grown acts to make the Top 25. Their competition was pretty stiff – up against classic performers who remain household names to this day – Elton John, Rod Stewart, Bryan Ferry, Billy Ocean, David Essex, the legendary Four Seasons and Chicago. 1975 had been just as stunningly successful for Australian acts, with Sherbet again securing number four spot for singles sales with *Summer Love*, followed by Skyhooks at number five with *Horror Movie* – a fitting number, I thought, to capture the previous six years of school!

Shirley Strachan and I would team up many years later to broadcast a number one rating Saturday night show on Radio 2

Triple M. To this very day our *Six Pack Saturday Night Party Show* holds the ratings record for a Saturday. Shirley was great to work with, had a great sense of humour and his famous falsetto belied the skill of a genuine radio pro. Together we had many laughs – on and off the air – and I was very saddened to learn of his death in a helicopter crash years later. He was the guy who put the Sky into the Hooks – he loved flying and I loved flying with him on our very popular show. He was still surfing on the success of his massive solo hit *Every Little Bit Hurts*, after going it alone as the other famous Skyhook Red Symons continued his career as the loveable villain on Channel Nine's *Hey Hey it's Saturday.* As Red teamed-up with Daryl Sommers, Shirley and I were having our own fun and just as much success every weekend.

These artists would provide the score for the movie in my mind about a successful DJ shooting for the stars!

There was one Aussie act that would become the famous of them all – and they would provide my anthem at the time: *It's a Long Way to the Top (If You Wanna Rock 'n' Roll),* released just before Christmas in 1975. Yes, the inimitable AC/DC became my rock gods and after actually meeting Bon and the Boys I was way beyond starstruck – I was *thunderstruck* long before that became the title of the hit from their 1990 album *Razor's Edge.*

To meet AC/DC backstage while working as the DJ at the Hurstville Civic Centre was a career defining moment. I knew I was in the presence of greatness as the band flew high on the success of two blockbusting album releases in 1975, *T.N.T* and *High Voltage.*

As I was to discover in many more subsequent brushes with celebrity the most successful performers happened to be the most unassuming – courteous and respectful while never appearing to take their stunning success for granted. AC/DC had been performing on the Aussie pub and club circuit since 1973. They had done hard yards in the smoke-filled, sticky carpeted dives that represented a mandatory tour of duty for any act hellbent on cracking the bigtime. AC/DC's meteor was about to illuminate the sky as one of the great hard rock bands of all time. You could not have anticipated that soaring trajectory in the humble confines of these Hurstville dressing rooms. It was February 1976 and with *High Voltage* set for global release with a reshuffled playlist I knew this serendipitous encounter would be an historic moment, in my life at least.

There I was shaking hands with the penultimate Rock God Bon Scott and the line-up of masterful musos that would catapult ACKER DACKER into the stratosphere of world music – guitarist brothers Angus and Malcolm Young, bassist Mark Evans and drummer Phil Rudd.

The playlist from that fateful night still rings in my ears!

Live Wire

She's Got Balls

School Days

It's A Long Way To The Top (If You Wanna Rock 'n' Roll)

High Voltage

The Jack

Can I Sit Next To You Girl

T.N.T.

Baby Please Don't Go

My 90-minute set as the DJ wasn't exactly a hard act to follow for AC/DC but I can't begin to explain the thrill of sharing the stage with these legends and meeting them as they tuned their instruments backstage. There he was – larger than life – Bon Scott warming-up the famous bagpipes of his Scottish heritage in rehearsing the higher notes of *It's A Long Way to the Top*. Bon was the complete gentlemen, never once showing any hint of condescension as he paused to introduce himself to this 'Neville Nobody' from the 'burbs, as if any introduction would ever be needed! They were a hot act, and they were a *class* act.

The meeting with AC/DC did wonders for my confidence. I wasn't imagining this encounter. It was real rocket fuel for my own ambitions to make music my life. I guess you could say I was a groupie on steroids, wanting to become heavily involved in the lives of my heroes by playing their music to the masses, to audiences much vaster than the crowded bourbon-soaked auditoriums of suburban pubs and clubs. But just as the boys from AC/DC knew and respected – I knew this face-to-face engagement with the punters were absolutely necessary rungs on the ladder, and I've never regretted a moment of those halcyon days.

By now I was fixated on becoming a radio announcer and connected with a community station in the inner western suburb of Concord to practice my studio craft. I was still living at home and spending every cent from my DJ gigs on investing in my future. One of the wisest investments was an audience with the undisputed king of radio voice training – the revered Max Rowley.

Max Rowley was a mentor for thousands of aspiring radio announcers, TV presenters and voice over artists and successful in his own right as the man behind the microphone in a range of television shows. "Max Rowley speaking...." was his famous sign off. I've always thought he was the inspiration for *King Wally Otto of the Soundproof Booth*, created by Australian comedy legends Roy Slaven and HG Nelson.

Most Australians would have heard Max's unmistakable dulcet tones on television, but he was rarely seen. I can recall a story in which he featured on *Simon Townsend's Wonderworld* as one of his few on-camera interviews. His voice could be heard in the TV soap *Sons and Daughters, The Dismissal,* as the voice over announcer for the 1980s games shows *It's A Knock Out,* and the top rating *Perfect Match,* hosted by Greg Evans.

His interview with *Wonderworld*'s Edith Bliss gave me a very clear reminder of just how stiff the competition was in trying to launch a career in professional broadcasting.

Max was telling Edith about voice over work specifically, in reminding me of the steepness of the climb that awaited me.

"Well, it really is difficult because you have to go through the process of becoming a radio announcer generally or an actor and from being an actor, then you reach as far as you can go. And then usually if you're lucky, someone says, 'Well, could you do a commercial for us?'

"There's only a handful of voice over actors we use regularly. Probably maybe more than a handful, about 10."

"The women are usually famous actresses like Judy Davis and people of that nature."

He had great advice on everything from how to back announce a song to reading a commercial with tips like this: "In a soft sell you use a much more convincing voice... motivating warm and sincere. But the hard sell is we cram so many words into the shortest possible period. Mostly 30 seconds are the ones that seem to really sell."

I never underestimated Max as the gatekeeper to any aspiring young radio announcer.

When asked what made a good, professional broadcaster he was in no doubt about square one.

"Well, I think a good voice is very important. You should always train your voice," he said. "You should train forever. There is no amount of research, training or courses you can do that will be enough. That said, you should train *while* you actively search for work. Don't train or practice without making some attempt to get work – to be forever training is fantastic. To be forever training without looking for work is disastrous!" The best presenters are usually the ones who will train more than anyone else!

When I wasn't paying for tuition from Max's radio school, I was buying expensive tapes, and studio time at the community station for recording scores of job applications at radio stations throughout Australia. Even then studio hiring was expensive, and I was paying up to $50 an hour to record my reels.

Max meanwhile was teaching me a lot more than how to 'spin the fantastic black plastic.' His lessons were invaluable and sometimes very simple, such as strong advice to never talk over the top of music and the finer points of projection and inflexion. He also had a keen eye for dedication and could tell I had it by the bucketful. I was zealous in my pursuit of a break and prepared to work anywhere to get a start, at one stage sending my tapes to far north Queensland, fully prepared to accept that the sweat from stinking humidity could be added to the blood and tears already expended on a countless number of applications. There were no audio files then of course to ping off in an email. Each application was accompanied with a reel of tape, and they weren't cheap. I still recall that sinking feeling of leaving the post office and wondering whether any of the parcels would ever be opened. At one stage I was so conditioned to rejection I wouldn't even bother opening the reply envelopes, knowing they would just thank me for the tape and add it to the bulging shelf storing scores of other wannabe jocks. I knew a phone call would be an obvious indication of genuine interest, so most of the letters went straight to the bin.

All the while my extended family continued to doubt my chances of ever getting the breakthrough that even I was beginning to consign to the realm of fantasy. But then came the phone call that changed my life. It was Max.

The general manager of 2LT Lithgow had phoned him for a recommendation of a cheap, young announcer willing to work an evening shift in a town on the western edge of the Blue Mountains, just 150 kilometres northwest of Sydney but in reality – an entirely new universe for this boy from the burbs.

The halo caused by the fog as it swirled around the dim yellow streetlamps of Lithgow was a stark reminder of just how far this place was from the 'bright lights of Vegas.'

If you ever wondered why Australia's first state was named New *South Wales* then our forefathers must have imagined a place like Lithgow. It had the atmosphere of a town from a moody D.H Lawrence novel. It was grim and gritty, sitting under a thick layer of black dust from the surrounding coal mines, like the town time forgot. It seemed only the cars had changed over the slow ticking decades in this humble corner of the world, set in a deep valley at the western end of the Bells Line of Road. It was once a bustling centre of industrial activity, with its own steel works and a small arms factory that made the famous *Lithgow Rifle*. The street names reflected the town's links to the war effort. There was *Rifle Parade, Ordinance Avenue, Bayonet Street, Lone Pine Avenue* and *Carbine St.* It was more an arsenal than a map! Consistent with the theme I arrived with my worldly belongings in the back of my trusty panel van on Tuesday January 4th 1977, determined to become the 'gun' new radio announcer, ready to enlighten locals on what songs were *shooting* to number one, with a *bullet* of course!

Apart from its reputation as a hard town with a history steeped in coal mining, steel milling and weapons manufacture Lithgow had also distinguished itself with the achievements of legendary Olympic athlete Marjorie Jackson, known as *The Lithgow Flash* after her victories in the 100 and 200 metre finals at the 1952 Helsinki Games. She would become one of the town's many notable citizens, including the highly successful Melbourne Storm NRL coach Craig Bellamy, the former head of the Australian Catholic Church Cardinal Edward Clancy, the sixth Prime Minister of Australia Joseph Cook, comedian John Doyle – AKA Roy Slaven, revered journalist Laurie Oakes, former Wallaby Rugby Union fullback Marty Roebuck, boxing champion Graeme 'Spike' Cheney, and more recently YouTube satirist Jordan Shanks.

I was interested to see an interview with John Doyle (the other half of Roy and HG) years later when he recalled his own anxiety from the presence of Catholic brothers in his schooling years at Lithgow.

He told the ABC's *7.30 Report*: "We were always troubled by getting the strap or getting the cane. It was wielded by the De La Salle Brothers. They were pretty swashbuckling in the way they used the strap. You couldn't get away with it today. So, we lived in fear and panic and that was the truth of the matter. The best way to slip through the cracks and to avoid punishment was to just be very shy and timid and do your work and try to stay unnoticed."

It's always strangely comforting and almost reassuring to learn others had processed their experience with the clergy in very similar stories of survival.

John Doyle of course became known as one of Australia's most loved comedians, and Lithgow dominated his Roy Slaven routine with rambling but completely fictional anecdotes about his character's heroics with the Lithgow Shamrocks rugby league side and the cinders running track at the local athletics field.

But back in 1977 I wasn't finding much to laugh about in Lithgow in my repeated attempts to settle into what seemed to be a very cliquey town.

By this stage, on the strong advice of Max Rowley, I had changed my name to Frank Vincent – an anglicization of my first two names, bowing to the insistence of the master, echoing the strategy of a boxing coach wanting to enhance his charger's marketability for professional bouts. It was my own version of *Goodbye Norma Jean* as Frank Vincent entertained those few people who weren't at home glued to their television sets. I figured my audience was mainly young kids wanting to keep up with the Top 40 and the drivers of those big trucks that would shake the studio windows as they rumbled past 2LT on Main St towards the Great Western Highway.

They were lonely nights in what amounted to a surreal existence, relieved by the calming influence of my lovely landlady Mrs Peck, and her mischievous son – my only real friend in the town. My attempts to blend into the community by dropping into the local pubs were invariably subverted by racist remarks. I remember one of the friendlier locals being interrupted by a red neck to be asked: "Why are you talking to this wog?" It seemed the new name of Frank Vincent wasn't providing enough cover! Then there was the time I was followed home before waking the next morning to discover all four tyres of my panel van had been slashed. While it wasn't hard to think I was literally going nowhere fast as I waited for roadside assistance, I remained determined to give this gig my all in the hope it would indeed become the steppingstone to bigger and better things in a capital city market, where the FM band was starting to evolve in a way that would revolutionise radio in the same way colour TV took television to whole new level.

But in the meantime, 2LT would become a great training ground, somewhere I could make my mistakes and learn without the whole world listening. It was far from a glamorous life, reading out race results and mastering the art of wrapping my tongue around all the quirky local names while trying not to offend the unforgiving locals with any clumsy mispronunciation of their beloved towns and villages. *The Vale of Clwydd* was particularly confronting. Turned out Clwydd is pronounced *clued* but I didn't have a single clue on how to spit it out, until the locals started spitting chips....

Throughout what could appear to be the drudgery of life as a humble country jock there was one stunning highlight of my time at 2LT – an opportunity to interview Michael Lee Aday, better known to the world as Meatloaf. CBS records was offering-up this rising American star for interview while promoting his iconic number one sensation *Bat Out of Hell.* Until then Meatloaf was relatively anonymous, after starting to build his name in the parts of Eddie and Dr. Everett Scott in the 1973 film production of *The Rocky Horror Show.* After overcoming my nerves at the prospect, I told the program director I could do the interview after all. It went smoothly and my confidence shot through the roof. Talk about a glowing entry into what had been a modest CV. I can still recall an odd answer to my question to Meatloaf about whether he thought *Bat Out of Hell* would be become number one. His reply dumbfounds me to this day. He said: "I believe anything is possible ... one day someone will pole vault 22 feet." I'm still scratching my head because last time I checked the record it was still only on 20.37 feet, or 6.21 metres. Regardless of his baffling prediction I had sharp sense that my career at least had taken a giant leap...

In the back of my mind, I was always determined to do Max

Rowley proud, and vindicate his judgement in recommending me in the first place. I also reminded myself – that in spite of a humble sixty bucks a week – I had the best of one might call fully subsidised hobbies, introducing the western Blue Mountains to the hits of 1977 in a year dominated by the likes of Julie Covington with *Don't Cry for Me Argentina*, Aussie Peter Allen with *I Go To Rio*, Andy Gibb's *I Just Want to Be Your Everything*, Boz Scaggs with *Lido Shuffle*, Smokie's *Livin' Next Door to Alice*, and ominously perhaps – *Help Is on Its Way* from the Little River Band. Then there was David Soul with *Don't Give Up on Us*. And I was never giving up on my dream of leaving Lithgow to take a shot at the big time.

CHAPTER 5

THE BIG SMOKE

With all respect to the parochial sensibilities held by the good folk of Lithgow one of the town's most appealing qualities was its proximity to Sydney. It took me little more than two hours to drive home to Fairfield, but it was tough going, especially in winter when the icy tarmac and heat-expansion corrugations of the cement Great Western Highway challenged even the most experienced motorists. Throw in more than a few speeding trucks, police patrols and variable speed limits adjusted for the many towns and hamlets along the way and the return to Sydney to catch-up with family and friends assumed the proportions of a major expedition. But it was a journey I undertook every week of my three-year stint in the coal mining town. I'm sure there was no shortage of things to do on Lithgow weekends but the friendliness and home cooking that awaited my regular returns to western Sydney was a vital recharge of my batteries, and further fuel for my ambition to crack a gig in the Big Smoke.

The smoke didn't come any bigger than the plumes shooting 24/7 from the huge stacks of Port Kembla in Wollongong, by now a

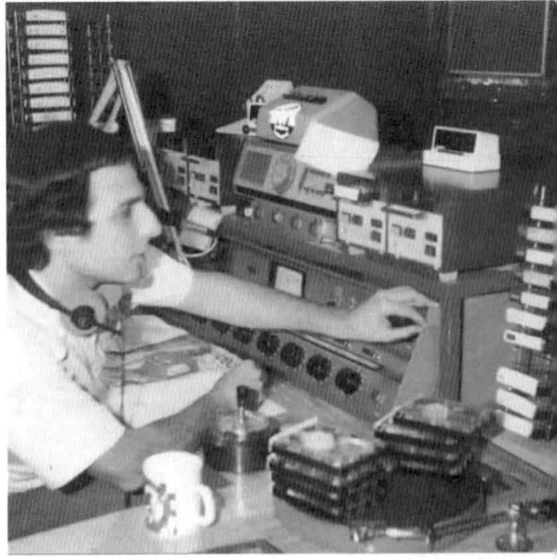

Vampire Hours — cup coffee at the read and the studio speakers cranked to make sure I'd stay awake till dawn.

The ratings winning team at 2WL — celebrating another victory over the Johnny-come-lately 2 Double 0.

two-station radio market thanks to the emergence of *2 Double 0* to compete with the incumbent 2WL. The latter was advertising for a midnight to dawn announcer and I threw my coal-dusted hat in the ring, fully prepared to switch from what used to be a small steel city to a much larger one that continued to thrive as one of Australia's industrial powerhouses. After Newcastle, Wollongong was the third largest city in NSW, and even closer to Sydney, just 85 kilometres south of the capital, on a narrow coastal plain snuggled between the Tasman Sea and a dramatic escarpment containing the coal that had long been the black blood of a city affectionately known to everyone as The 'Gong.

Wollongong was a genuinely multicultural city, attracting a variety of Europeans who had joined my family on the post war exodus to start life anew down under, so its appeal went beyond the summer-heated golden beaches making for my warm arrival after my brushes with racism inland.

Until now my familiarity with this dynamic city, like millions of others, had been confined mainly to *The Aunty Jack Show*, a zany TV comedy featuring a cross-dressing bikie who threatened to rip the arms from viewers who didn't tune into the ABC every week to watch the off-the-wall antics of the protagonist and his madcap mates, including a young Norman Gunston, soon to be made famous by Garry McDonald. My arrival coincided with the formation of the Illawarra Steelers Rugby League Club, ready to give Wollongong a deserved place on the national sporting map. I couldn't have known this at the time – the fun fact of the kid who won a competition to name the Steelers. Roger 'The Dodge' White steadily built a reputation as a solid radio journalist. He was a 'Walter Mitty' of sorts who also became the first Australian man to compete in luge at the Winter Olympic Games, featuring in the 1994 Lillehammer games in Norway. The Dodge went on to work as a commentator on the luge, bobsleigh and skeleton events in Channel 7's coverage of multiple Winter Olympics.

With the Lotto promos crew in Wollongong after my lucky numbers had already come-up to escape Lithgow and score a graveyard shift at 2WL.

Long before the Steelers were amalgamated with the St George Dragons the only things breathing fire in Wollongong were the smelters of the BHP steelworks, making for an imposing silhouette against the southern sky as if a corner of Germany's Ruhr Valley had somehow been airlifted and dumped in a sub-tropical paradise. For without the profile of the Port Kembla monolith Wollongong could easily have rivalled Honolulu for postcard perfection. The views of Wollongong on approach from the north are simply breathtaking. Majestic sums it up. From the coastal road, if you didn't know any better, you might be convinced you were somewhere on the Riviera. Where the coastal strip narrows to just 100 metres in the far northern suburbs the land is just wide enough for several hotels and restaurants affording a magnificent sweep of the ocean, with the waters stretching to the horizon dotted with the large cargo ships coming and going from Port Kembla with their payloads of black gold.

The 2WL studios were a stone's throw from Wollongong's famous North Beach, and I found a fantastic flat around the corner in Cliff Road, just near Wollongong Harbour. I was lightyears from the lonely frost-bitten streets of Lithgow and couldn't be happier even if a very unfriendly roster soon had me living the life of a vampire.

There's a good reason why the midnight-to-dawn gig is called the 'graveyard shift.' According to my research the term has its origins in the 1880s, when you only had to be in a deep coma to be pronounced dead, so the excavation of coffins would reveal scratch and claw marks on the inside of the timber lids from those who had regained consciousness before trying to fight their way out. To give the poor sods some chance of resurfacing a piece of string would be attached to a finger of the assumed deceased, and it would be connected directly to a bell above the ground for alerting the overnight cemetery worker to any need for an urgent rescue!

I'm happy to say my version of the graveyard shift was nowhere near as grim, but I'd be lying if I didn't disclose its darker moments, and the implications for one's health. For a start such a radical departure from the body's natural circadian rhythm creates havoc

Starstruck for the first time — and dwarfed by the giant Mick Fleetwood, the drummer of Fleetwood Mac on the Australian leg of the band's 1980 *Rumors* World Tour.

with the one's immune system and can lead to diabetes and weight gain. Such chronic threats weren't making themselves apparent to me as I grappled with the more acute problem of simply trying to stay awake. On cooler nights I'd play a song long enough to enable enough time for to slip outside for a reinvigorating hit from a brisk pace up and down in the bracing night air. Such a shift was beyond surreal, more like a permanent state of jetlag. Add the isolation and loneliness of sitting in a dark confined space for six hours and I was soon relating very strongly to Wollongong's coal miners, but at least they had workmates to keep them company. My conversations were confined to those night owls who would ring in with their various requests. Other callers were either drunk, stoned, stark raving mad or a combination of all three and I'd have my finger poised on the seven second delay button should any profanities or wilder conspiracies theories escape into the night air via the station's Port Kembla transmitter. At times it was a truly a case of "who am I and what am I doing here?" But I was determined to make the best of a gig at a station I hoped would be

Just when I thought I had bagged the photo of the night at the Fleetwood Mac Platinum Record presentation in Sydney 2WL music director Lee J Richards upstaged everyone by stealing a kiss from the wonderful lead singer Stevie Nicks.

the last rung on my ladder into a capital city market.

My interaction with the other staff was limited to notes from the program director and a brief exchange of courtesies with the breakfast announcer Steve 'Parso' Parsons before he jumped into my chair to wake the city up with his unique brand of *snap, crackle and pop*, as the old Rice Bubbles cereal ad used to go.

As you can well imagine such a radical roster doesn't make for an easy time of making friends in a city that only came to life when I sunk into belated slumber. I'd try to sleep between 8am and 2pm but for the most part that turned out to be overly ambitious, and by lunchtime in summer I'd find myself down at the beach trying to compensate for my depleted reserves of Vitamin D.

An unlikely candidate emerged as my first close friend in the 'Gong. My rival announcer on the same shift at 2 Double 0 Dave Carlson was weighing heavily into the dubious spirit of bitter competition with 2WL when I heard about a slur about how this Italian upstart should be running a pizza shop. I wasn't going to stand for that and confronted him. To his credit he was man enough to immediately apologise and we ended up becoming good buddies, relating very strongly of course to our unique custodianship of the wee small hours. We'd meet for breakfast and swap stories about the assortment of fruitcakes who had phoned-in overnight to keep us company in between songs. We'd also lament the quality of the music we were left to play – usually the B sides of the high rotation hits other announcers had the pleasure of spinning in the more lucrative daylight hours.

My circle of friends expanded to include a group of journalists of Wollongong's daily tabloid *The Illawarra Mercury*, which had been very kind in promoting me as 2WL's 'Elfin Wunderkind' in reference to my 5'7" frame! I'll be forever grateful to *The Merc*, as it was known, for ensuring my very first appearances in a newspaper's social pages. It's a stretch to think how anyone could know the name of a midnight to dawn announcer but that issue was settled one night when I was introduced to an audience at a local movie premiere only to receive a thunderous applause, more rousing than any recognition of the better-known names from our station. That reception provided an enormous boost to my confidence, crucial to any prospects of advancing to a larger radio market.

My love life meanwhile was blossoming in defying my unsociable hours. There was one occasion when a beautiful young lady known as *Red* appeared at my door to address any issues I was having with loneliness! Then there was Vicki Pollard, long before her namesake was made famous by those rogues from the hit British TV comedy *Little Britain*. I dated Vicki for a year. She was a great character, with a beauty matched by her great personality and ability to make me laugh. Vicki would always have a different funny story to tell about how we met, and her razor wit ensured there was never a dull moment.

Sleep was a constant priority; I would snatch a nap whenever I could. Even ten minutes of kip under a table would be enough to top up my batteries. Every time a friend suggested a meeting time for heading out – I would make it 15 minutes or half an hour earlier, and they knew I was only trying to buy even more windows for crucial shut eye. But I was young and energetic enough to battle through it, often relenting to a night out just like anybody else. I was keeping up my moonlighting as a DJ and became a fixture at several Wollongong pubs and clubs, still bursting to life with the constant procession of the same hot Aussie bands dominating the Top 40. My favourite was The Angels. Only AC/DC could match the capacity of Doc Neeson and the boys to ignite a venue with such rousing rock 'n' roll. I can still picture statue-like guitarist Rick Brewster barely blinking as he stood like a relic from Pompei as Doc bounced off the walls and floor with his own brand of melodramatic acrobatic choreography. It was real thrill to head straight to work and be the first to broadcast a review of the act I had watched just hours earlier, and then risk raising the ire of the program director by straying from the schedule of B side tracks to introduce one of the hits I had just witnessed.

There were some huge Australian and New Zealand acts on tour at the time when Splitz Enz beat all comers to produce the number one song for eight weeks in 1980 with *I Got You*, beating *Turning Japanese* from the Vapors, Queen's *Crazy Little Thing Called Love* and Pink Floyd's *Another Brick in the Wall.*

Life was good but looking back now I'm not terribly proud of how my growing confidence coincided with my diminishing reserves of humility. Upon deep reflection I simply wasn't mature enough to process my good fortune as graciously as I should have. I was becoming somewhat of a *big head.* A dream job considered by many to be ‘glamorous’, a steady stream of complimentary concert tickets, free records, and plenty of attention from the girls was lifting my feet from the ground when I should have parked my ego at the door. Confidence is one thing, but arrogance is quite another. Back then I thought it was either my way or the highway when I should have had greater respect for the opinions and the perspectives of others living outside my privileged world.

If anyone reading this was on the wrong end of my haughtiness – here is a belated ‘sorry.’ Life’s lessons have been tough enough since to bring me crashing back down to earth and temper my sentiment about those halcyon days with a good deal of regret. I can only blame my former self on a lack of maturity, and the ‘bullet proofness’ that is typical enough of any young Alpha Male with an exaggerated self-opinion!

I managed to muster some meekness though when I thought I was in the presence of greatness. Such was my opinion of 2WL music director Lee Jay Richards. I was in awe of Lee when he was a top jock on 2SM and he really took me under his wing. On one occasion Lee Jay had been invited to the presentation of a platinum record for Fleetwood Mac’s landmark *Rumors* album during their 1977 Australian tour. He asked me to come along, and I had the honour of meeting my first larger than life star – Mick Fleetwood – after the ceremony at the Cauldron night club. When I say larger than life – that’s no exaggeration. Fleetwood was a towering 6’6” and I looked like a veritable lilliputian standing beside him. But figuratively speaking at least the huge drummer was the last person on earth who’d speak down to anybody. I found him to be a somewhat gentle giant, and very humble about the band’s enormous success. It was a fabulous night, if not a little controversial as we hung with the group when the infamous henchmen who accompany such celebrities took issue with Lee when he pecked the cheek of the delightful Stevie Nicks. She didn't seem to mind at all but the contact was a little too close for the comfort of the bruisers who guarded her!

Although this 'goldfish' was being a little overfed in the Wollongong 'pond' I was still realistic enough to know I had a lot of work to do before I could pretend to mix it with those top rating announcers at the height of their powers in Sydney. There was none more accomplished then 2JJ legend George Wayne. He was the King of Kool, super smooth, an encyclopedia of cutting-edge music – all delivered with inimitable dulcet tones that could melt a box of chocolates. It was tempting to ignore Max Rowley's number one refrain on the importance of 'being yourself' on air when all I wanted to be was George Wayne. He was inspirational and highly motivational, regardless of whether he was actually aware of his profound impact on me. I had the honour of meeting him once in the ABC's William Street Kings Cross studios, and he was extremely grounded in the way truly talented people let their brilliance do all the talking. If my head needed shrinking – and there was really no question of that was after my Wollongong indulgences – George could guarantee it, as he set a great example of selflessness in taking the time to talk with this Wollongong Wannabe. He eventually introduced me to some record company executives to give me a real feel for the symbiotic relationship between influential announcers and the music industry.

Known by some as George 'Groover' Wayne, he would develop a cult following among listeners at a time when Sue Moses was blazing a trail for female announcers and JJ was continuing to unearth raw Aussie talent. George was a major player in promoting Australian talent. I remember being amazed by his interview via satellite with American legend Jackson Browne, starting with George inviting his celebrity guest to assess an Eric Clapton song he played. It turned out the phone line was dodgy but Browne liked what he could manage to hear – before an improving reception allowed him to be blown away by an AC/DC track, amusingly described by George at the time as 'punk rock.' I'm not sure what my old mate Bon Scott would have made of comparisons with Sid Vicious but I'm sure he would have been grateful for the huge plug to a very influential American artist.

So, there was AC/DC emerging again to stamp their act as world class, and on my very first trip to London Bon and the boys were busy taking the UK by storm.

Flying to London for the first time was much more than a rite of passage for me. It was a major leap in my maturity to land in a world city as a complete nobody and realise I had been having myself on as an entitled little shit in the antipodes! Growing-up in Fairfield I played junior soccer for Marconi and became a huge fan of English Premier League club Arsenal. It was always my dream to visit their north London stadium at Highbury – and I can still vividly remember literally pinching myself as I looked up at the famous Cannon marking the entrance to the headquarters for a team known as The Gunners. What a thrill.

I was swept away by the vibrancy of London, and the very real sense the UK was at the cutting edge of world culture and popular music of course, as the home of The Beatles, The Rolling Stones, Led Zeppelin, Pink Floyd, The Who, Queen, Bowie, Elton John, Sex Pistols and a seemingly never-ending list of megastars.

Of all the stars in this galaxy of legends a new Aussie 'sun' was shining brighter than them all at the time I was visiting the Old Dart and it was an electrifying AC/DC announcing their arrival on the world stage as the new dominant force of heavy rock 'n' roll.

I have a sharp recollection of swelling with pride and the goosebumps on my neck as I took my place in the heaving throng at the Hammersmith Odeon when the boys launched into exactly what I had expected – the transfixing opening beats of *Live Wire. The Jack* proved to be the highlight of the gig as the crowd screamed "Jack, Jack, Jack" in unison with Bon Scott. It was indeed a controversial song then and would be a prime target for today's custodians of the infamous 21st century cancel culture. I mean, seriously? Can you imagine how such a song could ever be published, let alone played on radio these straight-jacketed world of surly secularism. The song was nothing short of outrageous, even by the standards of a free-spirited swinging 70s London but that didn't stop the adoring crowds from singing along in an era when the Sex Pistols were in full offensive stride!

It was such a memorable trip, including visits to my spiritual home Italy, then Germany and France – in my first taste of globetrotting before visiting a total of 43 different countries until now. My spirits were soaring even higher after learning I had scored a new gig in Canberra. I'd be flying from the English capital to my country's own, joining a great mate who would become a lifelong friend after our meeting at Max Roley's academy.

CHAPTER 6

CAPITAL CAPERS

Poor old Canberra.

It's despised as a synonym for our loathed politicians, and variously derided as soulless – as grey as the faceless bureaucrats representing the largest slice of the population in the nation's capital. It's where the tax man resides along with the Governor General, representing the King – who for some unknown reason still wields the executive authority to sack our democratically elected Prime Minister.

Far from its noble aspirations of symbolising a unified Australia Canberra is in reality an enduring symbol of rivalries between NSW and Victoria. It was established in 1913 and two world wars since have done little to dilute the bitterness that lingers in Melbourne, which thought it should have been the nation's capital as the 19th century mercantile epicentre of Australia thanks to fortunes delivered by the Gold Rush. Less parochial Sydney was also bidding for the national seat of power as Australia's first major city and the tepid compromise was a slab of 'nowhere land' in the shadows of the Great Dividing Range on the Mongolo River, better known these days for the artificial lake named after the city's American architect in chief Walter Burley Griffin.

A friend recently quipped that he had finally discovered the beating heart of Canberra – the 24-hour Shell service station, opposite Manuka Oval on Canberra Avenue. "It's a hive of activity!" he reported with mock breathlessness. "Taxi and Uber drivers coming and going with their microwaved cheeseburgers and hot chocolate in paper cups! There's a real buzz there – 24/7 – it's the servo that never sleeps!"

But back in the early 1980s when a 24-year-old Frank Vincent was hosting the evening shift on Radio 2CC I was prepared to let the world believe it was more like Paris or New York! I had snared a job in capital city radio and was always ready to spruik I was working in not just any old capital city – but the *National Capital*! Deep down I knew Sydney would be the real definition of mission accomplished, but this job was filling my heart with the hope that a big metro market was a completely realistic scenario.

I scored the job on the recommendation of my great buddy from radio school Rob Duckworth. 'The Duck' as he would become known, was keen to have a mate share the pain and strain of living in the Southern Hemisphere's most boring capital city, and he only had to ask me once before lining-up my successful interview with station management.

Like 2 Double 0 in Wollongong 2CC was the Johnny Come Lately on the Canberra Radio scene, setting-up in 1975 to take on 2CA. It didn't take long to start dominating the incumbent and I like to think I had my own part to play in that success while getting my legs under the desk for the 6–10pm shift. After overcoming the jetlag of the return flight from London it was such a joy to be finishing work at a relatively civilised hour and getting to sleep by midnight. Well, that was the general idea at least. I had moved in with Rob and let's just say we worked hard and partied harder!

Broadcasting from a 5000-watt transmitter high above the summit of Black Mountain 2CC had a reach way beyond the borders of the Australian Capital Territory, with an audience covering wide expanses of southern NSW from the Victoria border all the way to Cowra in the NSW central west and as far east as the

Southern Highlands, just 100 km from Sydney.

The studios were located in a semi-rural area of Canberra's northern suburbs known as Gungahlin, and while I might have snared a job in capital city radio it didn't feel that way as I gazed out of the window at farm animals in a neighbouring paddock. It had all the appearances of working in a bush setting that made Main Street Lithgow look like a strip of Broadway. But aside from the fading embers of dusk in daylight saving time, it would be dark soon enough on my shift to forget the surreal scene afforded by the studio window and start focusing on the music.

It was a relief to be working outside the office hours at 2CC, minimising my contact with the program director at the time. To say the least I was not a huge fan, and nor did any of the other announcers rate him very highly. I remember how this executive blasted one of the announcers for not realising there was *dead air* while unwittingly playing a track on channel two, and not the channel required for the music to be broadcast. This error was known as 'backtracking.' The boss stormed into the studio and said: "Do you realise this song has been backtracking for the entire time it's taken me to walk from my office to the studio?" To which the jock replied: "Well, why didn't you fucking run?" It was one of the sharpest comebacks I've ever heard!

This same program director was always climbing into me for not sticking to 'the schedule' – a common enough gripe from those charged with the smooth day-to-day running of a radio station but this individual didn't allow any margin for the very same spontaneity and personality expected by management to help win the ratings. Sticking to the schedule – saying and playing exactly what was prescribed – was a constant source of tension, as any announcer would attest. The program directors fancy themselves as chess masters, and woe beholds any 'piece on the board' prepared to make its own moves.

I was sharing a house with my good mate *The Duck* – and as a couple of cocky young blokes on the town – they might easily have called me '*The Weave*' – because there was no shortage of *ducking and weaving* as we took it upon ourselves to ramp-up Canberra's nightlife with our various escapades in as many dens of iniquity, including the infamous Private Bin night club, or The Garbage Bin as it was called by disgruntled locals, undeterred by the occasional bikie bashing and drug deal. Our favourite dining was the fabled Portia's Chinese Restaurant in Kingston, where politicians and journalists would swap gossip and stories long before they were splashed on the front pages.

Canberra was also rewarding socially as a fixture on the touring circuit of international bands, and I got to see some great acts including the inimitable Ian Dury and the Blockheads.

They were fast building a reputation as trailblazers for live performances on the new wave circuit, starting with the success of their first single *Sex & Drugs & Rock & Roll*. This was followed by more hits including *What a Waste* and *Hit Me With Your Rhythm Stick*. Dury's lyrics were celebrated for their word play and witty observations of working-class life in Britain. Some of his words were *gut-busting* funny.

So, you can imagine my thrill when the PD asked me to interview Ian. Initially I was nervous. The enormity of his global celebrity hit me like....well – like *a rhythm stick!* But I was up for the challenge and soon as I was face to face with a legend, and he could not have been easier going. This was going to be my biggest interview since Meatloaf, but I was actually shaking hands with this superstar, not just talking across the crackle of an international phone line.

I was put at ease immediately upon discovering he was about my height, but he was still larger than life with his unmistakable swagger complete with a rich East London accent. Soon we were just chatting like old mates, and his tour manager was a terrific, an old school mate of Ian's who joined him on tours for sharing the inevitable good times of a colourful life on the road.

Ian was such a good sport and was only too ready to play along when I played one of his hits from the top selling *New Boots & Panties* LP called *Sweet Gene Vincent.* When the song was about to end on '*Gene Vincent*', I would cue Ian to back announce it and say '*Frank Vincent*' instead and he got it in one. No rehearsal. Just nailed it for one of my more magic memories. What a delightful guy.

As he was leaving the studios the station manager questioned me on whether I could assure him I hadn't put a child's call to air and belittled him the previous night. I swore to him that I hadn't and it turned out to be an announcer from our rival station, and the boy's mother was on the warpath. Ian – having tuned into this serious inquiry from the boss – said in his inimitable east London accent: "Are you in a spot of bovver with the Guv'na?" As I assured him of my complete innocence a young Rob Duckworth, long before his Triple M fame, approached Ian for an autograph. His genius for a winning one liner wasn't about to desert him as he wrote. "To Rob, who's job is with the gob." Priceless!

CHAPTER 7

MEGAHERTZ & MEGASTARS

The enormity of my move from Canberra to the towering giant of rock n roll radio Triple M was glaring from my very first day of work at the Sydney FM juggernaut.

I got out of the lift to see none other than legendary Roxy Music lead singer Bryan Ferry standing at reception, completely faithful to the legend of his sartorial splendour. He was the undisputed King of Cool, immaculate in a three piece suit and tie, with all the charisma, charm, and impeccable manners of a modern day Carey Grant. It was impossible to ignore his magnetic presence and extreme good looks as every female in the station found an excuse to make a spontaneous inquiry about the health of the receptionist and anybody else who happened to be in the vicinity. Ferry was touring to ride high on the success of Roxy Music's platinum block buster *Avalon*, and to borrow from the title of his tribute song to John Lennon it was easy to be *Jealous Guy* as the women flocked to him like seagulls.

After meeting Ferry briefly, I was in no doubt Triple M was like Disneyland for DJs. Here I was in the presence of greatness, an iconic performer once described as an "art object who should hang in The Tate." Beats hanging in London's Tower, I guess. Like most superstars with little left to prove Bryan was completely charming and unaffected. He'd be the first in a long line of rock Gods and other A list global celebrities I had the pleasure of meeting in Sydney radio's new tower of power. As Bryan was waiting to be interview 10am–2pm announcer Trevor Smith was chatting in the studio with British talk show king Michael Parkinson. And this was the first morning of day one. They called this *work*.

After meeting Bryan Ferry I couldn't help but reflect on my Lithgow days and the excitement of having Meatloaf on the line for a live interview. Then there were the flashbacks of meeting Bon Scott and Ian Dury. This career was already one helluva ride and I wasn't going to be disembarking anytime soon. So many are preoccupied with the *length* of life, but I've always been much more interested in its *depth*, and I was taking the deepest of dives!

Triple M was already boasting the who's who of Sydney commercial radio, but we were nobodies compared to the passing parade of global megastars who graced us with their presence. There's something infectious about being amid true greatness, and it's also very humbling. I was also struck by the amazing humility of the bigger names. Their minders are trained to interrupt a conservation between a star and a stranger if the conversation seems to be going a little long. Such was the case when a security guard noticed a lengthy chat with the great Phil Collins, touring Australian for the first time as a solo performer after his band Genesis disbanded.

It turned out Phil loved soccer, or football as it's correctly called in his native England. I had recently seen him in a crowd cutaway in coverage of a Tottenham game at Whitehart Lane, and assumed he was a Spurs fan. I was wrong. He'd only grabbed a ticket because he was aching to see a game, before flying out.

To my great delight he told me he was also an Arsenal fan, and the banter flowed from there. It were as is if he was homesick, and I was providing an instant cure with my enthusiasm for the beautiful game. But at this stage his hefty sidekick was none the wiser, and barged in to wind me up. When the big fella discovered we were wrapping about the EPL he joined in – and nothing else seemed to matter for Phil. He went on to share how he was "embarrassed to be rich". He spoke of his simple upbringing as the son of an insurance agent, introduced to music when his father bought him a toy drum kit at the age of five, two years before he won a talent quest with a rendition of *The Ballad of Davy Crocket.* The man I met had come a long way from his childhood in the London suburb of Putney and was at the height of his powers on the Australian leg of a world tour to promote his chartbusting *No Jacket Required* album. He'd go on to win a Grammy Award for *Against All Odds,* the theme song of the same-named romantic movie. But for ten special minutes in a Bondi Junction radio station he could escape the surreal world of fame and all its trappings, and become a temporary *bestie* with a fellow Gunners nut from the sunburnt streets of Sydney's suburban west. I got a strong sense that he craved the normality of a simple life in the manner of an almost accidental star, who had shot to an altitude that must surely have been beyond his wildest dreams. Maybe that was the X factor involved in his success, a subtle signal to the punters that he was one of them after all. Of all the big names I've met over the years Phil Collins still stands head and shoulders above them as a true champion, with the sincerity and integrity to match his enormous talent.

Phil was one of those rare birds who could drum and sing, like Don Henley from The Eagles and Queen's brilliant Roger Taylor, who was adding the high notes to the British supergroup's famous inimitable harmonies while occasionally somehow managing to upstage Freddie Mercury by belting out his anthem for rev heads *I'm In Love with My Car.* I got to meet Roger and the supremely talented Queen guitarist Brian May on their 1986 tour of Australia, that followed their blow-all-comers-off-the-stage hijacking of Bob Geldof's legendary *Live Aid* concert at Wembley. I never met their flamboyant front man, but through my good mate Duckworth I was fortunate to enjoy the company of Freddie's colleagues Roger and Brian. It must have been challenging to be so talented while living in the imposing shadow of Freddie Mercury, who constantly demanded and commanded all the on- and off-stage attention with his god-like presence. This was never more evident than the time I was sharing a beer with Brian at The Sheaf Hotel in Sydney's Double Bay.

A band was setting-up for that night's entertainment and Brian approached one of the roadies, offering to play. This yobbo said, and I'll quote him verbatim. "Fuck off mate. We're a professional band – you can't just rock up here and expect to play!" Somehow this tool must have been among the three people and a solitary cat on the planet who had never seen the *Bohemian Rhapsody* film clip! Brian was very sporting about the rejection, and I'm sure he'd be dining out on the story until this very day.

Rob Duckworth started to build a reputation for drawing the big names of world rock into studio A for his drive shift, and as a floating announcer and sports reporter my opportunities for such career highlights were somewhat more limited, so you can imagine my delight when the program got to me to fill a morning shift for an ill Stuart Cranny and interview the lead duo from The Manhattan Transfer – the supersmooth vocal group featuring the super talented Janis Seigel and Tim Hauser. Both were thoroughly delightful, and I formed an immediate bond with them in an interview they later described as the best they'd ever done. I was chuffed with such high praise, but the chemistry between the three of us was seamless, and they were quite open with their appreciation by giving me a hug and a kiss as they left – and two seats bang in the middle of the front row of the Sydney Entertainment Centre for their performance that night. Their brand of a cappella swing mixed with pop and rhythm and blues was not exactly standard fare for the typical Triple M listener but anyone tuning-in would have been left in no doubt about their class and talent. I've never heard any live performers produce such a stunningly accurate account of their recorded material. This supremely slick outfit were in the groove and didn't skip a single beat with their replication of pristine studio quality hits including *The Boy from New York City, Smile Again, Tuxedo Junction, Don't Let Go, Chanson d'Amour, Twilight Zone* and *Route 66.* After winning no less than 11 Grammy awards I wasn't in the least not surprised to see The Manhattan Transfer enter the Vocal Group Hall of Fame.

It's not every day you walk into the office and see David Robert Jones hanging around the place. But there he was! AKA David Bowie – a strikingly handsome guy with impeccable manners and a polish that defied the image from his early days as the edgiest of glam rockers. Long before Madonna turned reinvention into her own artform, Bowie was showing as many if not more chameleon qualities, appearing for this Australian tour in the early 1980s. The greasepaint and the red spiky hair were long gone and Bowie re-emerged in 1983 with whiter than white straightened teeth, impeccable pastel double breasted suits with cropped blonde hair and a tan. This time Bowie was rebelling against his former self maybe in a blatant but nonetheless striking shape shift to become more commercial and seal the deal no doubt for a breathtaking new contract with EMI rumoured to be worth a staggering 17 million British pounds.

By now we have well and truly established the frenetic madhouse that was Triple M's Studio A. If the station was a zoo – this was the main cage, the smoke-filled setting for the more exotic exhibits where the lions, elephants in the room, egos, hyenas, actual tigers, barking traffic girls and black rats all gathered for a daily orgy of outright insanity.

It's difficult to imagine how the atmosphere could become crazier, right? Wrong. Add one Robin Williams to the mix and studio one is going right over the edge. The motor-mouthed comic genius took the joint by storm in a scintillating exchange with our own resident wit Doug Mulray, and suddenly all hell was threatening to break loose. Williams was in town to promote his hit 1987 movie Good Morning Vietnam, in which he plays zany on-base radio announcer Adrian Cronauer in Saigon. For his mastery of the role Williams went on to earn an Oscar nomination, announcing his arrival as a big screen star, before establishing his Hollywood bankability with lead roles in *Dead Poet's Society* and *Mrs Doubtfire*.

When I met Robin he was still best known for his TV role in the 1979 Emmy Award-winning *Mork & Mindy*, and most familiar to Australian audiences for his portrayal of a quirky alien trying to adjust to the earthly mundanities of life in sleepy Boulder Colorado. On this day at Triple M Williams seemed to be reincarnating all his off the wall characters, including Mork and any number of alter egos he had adopted as a master of improvisational stand-up comedy. Add Uncle Doug Mulray to this heady mix and a fast rising flood of tears was threatening to saturate the floor of level 25.

But I wasn't seeing the funny side of this day as soon as I arrived at work only to be collared by one of the guest's henchmen, warning me to stay away from the star. I was mightily offended and reminded this goon that I was in fact attending my place of employment. I couldn't get over the hide of this brute, visiting my workplace to throw his considerable weight around as Williams ran around the joint in full *Mork* mode, bouncing off the walls and accosting staff with his manic rants.

Unlike his hulky hired help Williams was down-to-earth and

very affable, politely rebuffing my suggestion that *Mork & Mindy* may have touched on a sporting theme. In the end, my on air intersection with this Hollywood great was quite narrow, as he continued to dominate the Mulray Bunch show by recreating his character from *Good Morning, Vietnam* in a display of art imitating life imitating art and so on! Williams blew the VU metre into deep red and threatened to bend the sound levels needle in its enclosed glass case as he bellowed his famous "Goooooooooooooooooooood morning Vietnam!"

Doug was clearly inspired by his lightening exchanges with Williams and was showing the world he could go blow for blow with one of its funniest men. I have a very sharp recollection of the tableau as I sat less than a metre away from Mullos and Williams going hammer and tong against the backdrop of spectacular Sydney Harbour glistening in the early morning sun. It was another moment to pinch myself hard, again juxtaposing the sight with the silent, anonymous streets of my upbringing, wondering how on earth I managed to land in such a special place.

As the appearance of Williams showed, the procession of megastars arriving at Sydney's supreme radio station was not always featuring musical performers. It seemed like any big name visiting Sydney would make Bondi Junction a mandatory port of call, with their promoters knowing they would have no larger megaphone to promote their talent to a young, cashed-up audience.

When Planet Hollywood opened its new restaurant in George St they flew in Sylvester Stallone for the occasion, and I struggle to recall being in the presence of a bigger star than this heavyweight of the *Rocky* and *Rambo* franchises. Unlike his aggressive on screen personas, Sly was the literal representation of the *gentle* man, unwaveringly polite in a way that suggested he was constantly mindful of his humble beginnings in New York City. He was so obliging he didn't hesitate when promos producer Steve Hunt asked the star if would mind recording station promos as the records played in between in his chats with Doug. There was no prima donna occupying the soul of this self-made superstar. He was pure class and couldn't do enough to please his hosts.

Doug was a huge Monty Python fan, so was absolutely thrilled to find himself interviewing the charming and extremely funny Michael Palin when he lobbed in Sydney to promote *Monty Python's Meaning of Life*. The Python co-founder was a champion, and fully prepared to participate in the whacky spirit of things while recalling the hilarity and controversy of making *Monty Python's Life of Brian*, the sublimely funny feature film that catapulted the Pythons to world-wide fame, and of course – infamy in the God-fearing deep south of America. Palin was a delight. He arrived at the Ms without any entourage or attitude and showed an enormous amount of respect for radio station staff, displaying not a splinter of the haughty affectation for which so many other giants of entertainment could be so notorious.

I wasn't meeting all the huge names within the confines of Triple M. I was a regular on the nightclub circuit in Kings Cross, which was in roaring contrast to the boring, vanilla monument to gentrification it has become in recent years. One of the more exclusive after dark haunts was Bennys, where guests would queue outside a door with a small sliding panel that enabled the door attendants to size up the wannabe guests and assess their coolness or fame. As a regular with Triple M cred I was always waved through, but would have to do some fast talking to negotiate the entrance of any companions were considered by the scrutineers to be 'Neville Nobodys.' The screening was tough for a reason. The other guests could include celebrities of world fame, and their protection from 'the great unwashed' was paramount, often ensured by their presence in roped-off areas of the club or private rooms. On one such evening I was privileged to meet Led Zeppelin lead singer Robert Plant. We were chatting about his bemusement over how the BBC had voted Zep's *Stairway to Heaven* as the greatest rock song of all time. Plant had his own thoughts on the matter, and I weighed in with my belief that *Whole Lotta Love* should have got the gong.

Australia in the 1980s was a firm fixture on the calendar of any giant act touring the planet, and I would have the thrill of meeting U2's Bono (who congratulated me on my 'superb taste' after being introduced as an ardent fan by Rob Duckworth), the impossibly handsome Jon Bon Jovi, and the charismatic lead singer of The Police, Gordon Sumner AKA Sting. I will forever remember the spectacle of the unassuming Sting walking out of an elevator at the Sebel to be swamped by adoring female fans and taking it all within his stride.

But rising above all these great acts was inimitable Pink Floyd. Everything they play is brilliant, every stroke of a keyboard deliberate, with lead singer Dave Gilmour setting the highest of standards for flawless live performances that dazzled audiences with an unerring faith to the unique sound of their original records. Many rock fans enjoy a variation from the LP releases and love live performances for that reason – but Pink Floyd treated their masterpieces with the due reverence they deserved. Nothing was considered complete until it was perfect. Their live rendition of *Run Like Hell* was the most sensational conclusion to a concert in rock n roll history. The staging and the lighting was breathtaking, exceeded only by the superb music of course. I've been to more than 5000 concerts – and daylight finishes second after the Floyd finish. I had the tremendous pleasure of attending seven of their Australian concerts after promoter Paul Dainty recognised my contribution in promoting the tour through a live interview with Keith Williams at Melbourne's 3 Triple M. I was obviously raving about the concert and the promoters appreciated my enthusiasm, and invited me to attend as many Floyd concerts as I wished. Needless to say, I embraced this generous offer, and attended three Sydney concerts, one in Melbourne, two in Brisbane – and all of this was on top the first time I saw them live in London.

Around this time I then had the honour of reacquainting myself with Jim Kerr, the lead singer of Scottish supergroup Simple Minds. Kerr was among the most impressively sincere celebrities I have ever met. I had interviewed him in Canberra two years before we met again – and in the true spirit of SM's smash hit from *The Breakfast Club* movie, Jim *'Don't You Forget Me'* Kerr did in fact *remember* me – by name! "Frank!" he said with a beaming grin. "We met in Canberra? Right?" We did indeed, and I recall marvelling at the memory of a man who would have met tens of thousands of people while circling the globe 20 times over in the interim. I was certainly flattered to linger in the memory of such a major star.

Simple Minds was a massive act at the time, and often compared in style and substance to Australia's own INXS, now threatening to surpass AC/DC for Aussie supergroup status. I felt like I was on a personal journey with INXS, given their frequent visits to the studios, that came with invitations to see them perform in small, strictly word-of-mouth 'inner sanctum' concerts at venues such as the Mosman Hotel. I recall one night at that pub in 1982 where Hutch and the boys previewed their breakthrough album *Shabooh Shoobah,* which foreshadowed their arrival on the world stage after entering the American Billboard 200. The lads were now shooting for the stars and I was lucky to see them blast off from the launch pad.

CHAPTER 8

THE ORIGIN OF A SPORTING LIFE

By now you may well be curious about how exactly the theatre of Doug Mulray's labyrinthine mind could have concocted 'the inflatable sport reporter.' It was obscure to say the least, and not exactly open to anybody's intuition, way beyond the wildest of guesses...

The fact is the whacky title has its origins in arguably the most famous Australian sporting event of them all – the Melbourne Cup.

One morning Uncle Doug – the motor racing devotee – was showing little patience for the great race of the *equine* variety. Like all geniuses Doug was prone to the odd mood swing, and on this day he was dark on the world generally. He very reluctantly followed the program schedule to interact with the listeners about the Melbourne Cup and could only cope by stamping the occasion with his usual brand of borderline banter, that would be subjected to the scrutiny of that holier than thou lot trying to police our sensibilities and humour these days. By today's standards Mulray's quip about the Melbourne Cup would be the subject of a code complaint to the Australian Communications and Media Authority, from anyone offended by the use of *rhyming slang*. Mulray decided to make his listeners explain to him the meaning of 'a horse's hoof.' When one humourless – or politically correct – member of the audience phoned-in to volunteer his theory for the answer as some sort of horseshoe Doug cut him off, threw his headphones down and stormed out of the studio. He was in no mood for anyone not tuned into his unique brand of off-colour humour.

For someone who generated so many belly laughs from day to day there was nothing avuncular about Uncle Doug as he decided to get up and go mid show, convincing himself an earlier than usual lunch was the answer to elevating his low spirits. It sounds like an audacious fit of pique, but it was all part of his act, in which I had been a relatively small fixture until this morning when I was suddenly called upon to sit on the other side of the console and finish Doug's shift. He wasn't coming back any time soon and as they said in the grand tradition of the entertainment game – 'the show must go on.'

As it turned out I managed to steer the Mulray Bunch show back into the harbour without skipping a beat, and my rescue efforts received wide and warm recognition from the general manager to the program director and other impressed staff.

Somewhat bemused by the high praise directed my way Doug said words to the effect of: "Well how about that? I walk out and they just grab Frank and blow him-up like an inflatable radio announcer." It was classic Doug. His mantra – always found scrawled on paper above the studio door – was: "Be preposterous". He was unwaveringly faithful to his mission statement, and for better or worse, I acquiesced to his demands to follow this instruction to the letter.

When I resumed my usual chair in the studio Mullos would always announce me as 'the inflatable sports reporter.' My new title could have been mistaken as a monument to Doug's rebellious and impetuous antics but it really did launch me to a whole new level of recognition, and soon *Frank Vincent* would be taking a back seat to my new alter ego. Listeners and sports people alike would instantly relate to me as 'the inflatable sports reporter' and I was getting a small taste of the fame with which Doug had long since been monotonously familiar. Yes – I was surfing in the white water of a comic genius but thrilled to be jumping on the wave every day!

With all the laughs came the serious business of journalism, and increasingly I was leaving the studio to mix it with the biggest names in Rugby League, Union – and curiously – motor racing. Those who researched the tastes of the Triple M listeners determined that a large cohort of Rev Heads was prominent in our audience between the ages of 25 and 39.

Mulray was already mad about motor racing, and this research on rev heads only served to seal my fate as the one who had to provide regular updates on every screech of the tyre from Formula One to what was then known as the Bathurst 1000 race for production cars. But my destiny to cover motor racing had been written in the stars from my time at Lithgow, just a 40 minute drive from the fabled Mt Panorama, where the giants of Australian motor racing would gather every year, mainly to settle the score between Holdens and Fords. I wasn't attracted to one make or the other, but as a huge fan of Peter 'Perfect' Brock I guess I found myself in the GMH camp as replaced his signature 05 Torana with various incarnations of his HDT Commodore. Consistent with his nickname Brock was the perfect gentleman, and always made time for Triple M in acknowledging the station's support of his sport extended far beyond coverage of the 'silly season' – the title traditionally afforded the gap between the football grand finals and the first of the Test cricket matches. *Brocky,* as he was also known, displayed none of the affections one might be quick to associate with someone with an enormous national profile, and I still remember the warmth and trust he displayed when I flew to Melbourne to interview him once at his beautiful home. With the recording complete he had to leave straight away and told me to make myself and home and let myself out. His heroics on Conrod

Straight were admirable enough – but that episode of sincere hospitality looms large in my memory of a thoroughly decent and unpretentious character, who took none of his fame for granted.

My coverage of motor racing for Ms led to my association with many other legends of the sport, including triple World Drivers Formula One Champion Sir Jack Braham and Alan Jones, who won the same title in 1980. Alan always laughed when I would make a big show of clearing a path for him in the motor racing crowds. "Ladies and Gentlemen – please make way for Mr Alan Jones!" For some reason that never ceased to tickle him.

But in all honesty my most valuable relationship in motor racing was with none other than Doug Mulray. He was absolutely crazy about cars and had a collection of Jaguars to prove it. In fact, they often featured when driving hardball contract negotiations with management. In his determination to receive maximum reward for his status as the goose that laid Triple M's golden eggs Doug invariably pointed to the fact that his stable of Jags was in ongoing need of *expansion*. By the end of his time at the Ms I thought he could easily have opened his own dealership! It was our shared passion for motor sport that bonded us in a way that Doug afforded me constant protection as a valued member of his team. Whenever the vultures started to circle me in the event of any transgressions on my behalf Doug would quickly rubbish any talk of my replacement. For as long as Doug ruled the roost at Bondi Junction my job was assured, but unfortunately, I wasn't mature enough at the time to keep my ego in check and like many young blokes in the media I assumed a certain level of bullet-proofness when in fact my bravado was becoming the source of great resentment among those who were only humouring Doug's support for his inflatable sidekick. As it turned out there were plenty lining-up to *deflate* me – for good, but more on that later.

Triple M's great support of Rugby League came with a risky twist. As I mentioned earlier David 'Maroon and White' was a proud Manly supporter, who enlisted Sea Eagles stalwart Paul 'Fatty' Vautin as a regular paid guest. Mullos was a northern beaches boy, and lifelong supporter of Manly, but this team happened to be the most hated in the competition. They were the derided 'silvertails' who 'bought their way to success' by poaching players from the clubs of the working class, such as the South Sydney Rabbitohs and the Western Suburbs Magpies. And this was the potential problem: most of Triple M's devoted listeners followed the battling teams of Sydney's inner and western suburbs and Triple M was aligning itself with a despised enemy, long before the Brisbane Broncos and Melbourne Storm arrived to assume their place as the NRL cartoon villains.

Along with motor racing the petrol head listeners of Triple M also loved Rugby League, a snug fit for their musical tastes, that usually meant Cold Chisel would be guaranteed high rotation on the station's playlist.

As a childhood fan of the Parramatta Eels I was lucky enough to be bathing in the glow of their great premiership success in the 1980s, at a time when State of Origin was replacing the grand final as the pinnacle of the sport.

As David White was fond of saying – the "smell of the liniment was imminent" (a line I went on to 'borrow' on many occasions) as I prepared to cover my very first trip to the infamous cauldron of Origin hostilities – Lang Park. This battleground was Rugby League's version of Waterloo, although I'm pretty sure even Napoleon and the Duke of Wellington would baulk at the ferocity of what I was about to witness – the most bitterly fought series in the history of the iconic interstate competition. By the end of three games only six points separated the teams.

It was hard not be intimidated as a New South Welshman as I walked into Lang Park for Game One of the '91 series. Balmain star Benny Elias was skippering the Blues and King Wally Lewis was leading the Maroons as he set out on his swansong as Origin's most celebrated combatant.

At the time Lang Park had a capacity of only 32,000 but it sounded like there was triple that as the fans crammed into the steeply raked grandstands flanking the pitch. You could cut the roaring air with a knife, and many a NSW fan was careful not become too conspicuous should the battle on the ground spread into bleachers. I was concentrating on keeping my head down.

The tension of this occasion wasn't going to be relieved. It was a nail biter and 64 minutes had passed before Queensland opened the scoring with a blockbusting effort from centre Mal Meninga, who charged straight through Greg 'Brandy' Alexander and Andrew 'ET' Ettingshausen to score. By the time Laurie Daley scored NSW's only try it was too late – and Meninga's goal kicking proved the difference as the home side secured a 6–4 victory. This had been a battle of attrition, a masterclass of percentage football characterised by the sort of ferocious tackling that saw Queensland's debutante fullback Paul Hauff denied man of the match honours when he was pulled out of the game with a dislocated shoulder.

With victory assured the atmosphere of what had been the most ferocious of arenas suddenly melted into the warmth of unbridled celebration. The affection of the crowd and players alike was unforgettable as the Maroons walked around the ground to thank the legions of delighted fans. Wally Lewis proved himself to be no 'germ-a-phobe' when one punter threw him a can of Four-X beer.

Showing all his customary dexterity the King seemed to catch it and skull it in one motion, to the disbelief of teammates who told him: *"Anything could have been in that tinnie!"*

Game 2 was bound to be bitter. Determined to square the series the Blues coach Tim Sheens drew upon his close relationship with NSW enforcer Mark Geyer from their days at the Penrith Panthers. Losing for NSW was never going to be an option and Geyer or MG as he was known was being primed as the heat seeking missile that would blow the Maroons apart. I got an exclusive hint of Geyer's special mission when he defied a media ban, jumping over furniture in the dressing room and grabbing my microphone to declare. "MG is going to have a big one!" He wasn't wrong.

The big man took his brief very seriously, perhaps too seriously, as he tore into the opposition like a man possessed, culminating in his infamous tangle with the King himself. It all started when Geyer shook the foundations of the Sydney Football Stadium with a bone rattling tackle on Maroons hooker Steve Walters. The game erupted just before halftime after Queensland prop Andrew Gee rushed to his dazed teammate's aid. Geyer was in the thick of second half hostilities when his forearm crashed into the head of Paul Hauff, returning with his shoulder now back in place after Game 1. To the shock of many, and the utter disbelief of the northerners Geyer was not sent off by Queensland referee David Manson, and an intact NSW side went on to win 14–12 after a Ricky Stuart cut-out pass sent centre Mark 'Sparkles' McGaw over the line to lock the scores at 12–12 six minutes before fulltime and Michael O'Connor's conversion. When Geyer was swamped by media in the dressing room, he told his father all the attention must mean he had been made *Man of the Match*. Nothing could be further from the truth. The journos were wanting his reaction to the news he'd be suspended for five weeks in an instant adjudication of his head high tackle on Hauff.

The stage was now set for an historic decider back at Lang Park and the 12th of June 1991 would go on to embed itself in Rugby League folklore. As NSW's misfortune would have it Game 3 was to be the final origin appearance of Wally Lewis but not a single soul could have known his home ground would reach unprecedented heights of parochial fervour just ten minutes before fulltime when the ground announcer revealed this Origin would be The King's last. On game day Lewis had received the news that his daughter Jamie-Lee was deaf – and he instantly decided that family would be firmly first. In the mirror image of Game 2 a Dale Shearer try would lock the scores at 12–12 late in the second half, and Meninga would repeat the feat of Michael O'Connor by booting the winning conversion to set up a fairy-tale farewell for the legendary warhorse Lewis.

I had just witnessed what I still consider to be the greatest State of Origin series of all time and even as a New South Welshman I could not help but me moved by the spectacle of Lewis saying his goodbyes, holding the hands of his young sons Mitchell and Lincoln on his farewell lap of a ground later replaced by a Suncorp Stadium, that now welcomes visitors at its entrance with a bronze statue of the five eighth who once ruled over every blade of its hallowed, scorched turf.

Back at Triple M Doug Mulray was looking to deliver on his threat to leave the station if the management didn't agree to acknowledge his ratings winning ways with the reward he thought to be thoroughly deserved. He kept insisting there were plenty more Jaguars to purchase and wouldn't budge. His view of management had always been cynical – and he was never afraid to broadcast his bemusement with the bosses to the world. I remember him opening the mic to tell listeners: "there must me a board meeting here today – I just saw a sacrificial lamb being carried into the boardroom." He was convinced the station's new owners had turned the studios into a bean counter's office with microphones. He once took matters into his own hands by handcuffing a time and motion consultant to the steel bracket of a fire extinguisher before leaving for a long lunch with Dave Gibson.

Doug never missed a chance to taunt the management – referring to one executive as 'Poison Ivy' and another CEO as 'Prince Valiant' in a dig at his straight fringe and helmet like haircut.

The executives were not the only ones getting a ribbing from Doug. One of his favourite pastimes was to tease afternoon announcer Ron E Sparkes about his age. Sparkes hated it.

One day I walked into Studio A and Ron E was cross-eyed, flipping a pen into the air catching it during a song, and appeared to be very upset.

"Why the grumpy face?" I inquired.

"If Doug makes one more crack about my age I'll start giving it back to him!"

Doug could never resist an opportunity to swoop on anything related to the elderly, and somehow reference Ron E to whatever geriatric theme happened to bounce into his mischievous mind. It didn't matter whether it was walking sticks, wheelchairs, or metal railings in the toilet – Doug would find a way to include Ron E in the scene. But the butt of these jokes had no way of appreciating the humour.

I wasn't afraid to stir Ron E either. He took his craft pretty seriously, and I guess that's what made him such a juicy target. When he was winning the drive slot I would ring-up on the listeners line and say: "Ron E – it's working!" he was happy to take those calls but could have been forgiven for not appreciating me after he slumped to number four in the ratings and I'd still ring and say: "Ron E – it's *not* working!" Others, meanwhile, were not appreciating my hijinks.

As Doug's emotional ties to Triple M were being stretched – so was the patience of my bosses. I had been too blinded by my ego to realise my own days were numbered there, but unlike Doug I wasn't to have any say in my future. I was told by one of my few trusted colleagues to watch my back, that the new program and news directors were staging monthly interviews for my replacement. So, from that moment I started canvassing other career options, meeting with 2UW programming supremo Cherie Romaro to discuss the possibility of pulling a few shifts on her successful AM station.

In the meantime, I was determined to push on with my career as a sports journalist. I was proud of my vast network of contacts in sport. From players, to their managers, champion racing drivers and the administrators of both rugby codes I had built-up an enviable list on speed dial.

Doug was also a big fan of Rugby Union, and David White would introduce my reports in his typical style. "Now here's Frank Vincent – slipping on his houndstooth jacket with leather elbow patches" to update us on the world of the *Rah Rahs*, as Rugby players were known due to the perception, or more likely the *reality* of their association with elite private schools.

I met some great people in the world of Rugby, and none more impressive than Mark Ella. At the time of printing he held a record for being the only Wallaby to score three tries against the home countries thanks to a missed tackle from England's Eddie Butler. He still toasts Eddie to this very day.

I wasn't always cosy with the big names of Rugby. David Campese never forgave me for my scathing review of his infamous, disastrously bad pass in the 1989 game against the British Lions. Weeks later he brushed me one night at Randwick Rugby Club at Coogee, but luckily Mark was there to lift my spirits. He became a great mate. I introduced Mark to my mentor and Rugby tragic Doug Mulray, and I'll never forget how I once joined Mullos in sculling champagne one morning from the Web Ellis Trophy – after the Wallabies won the World Cup in England. The boys brought the giant gong into the Triple M studios, and as you can imagine it could hold plenty of bubbles, and there wasn't a drop left by the end of another raucous shift. This breakfast show was right up there with the more outrageous performances from the Mulray Bunch and I was playing my part in the madness by doing justice to Peter Finch from the movie *Network*. You may recall the scene in that film when Finch's news anchor character tells viewers to "stick your heads out the window and yell- I'm as mad as hell and I won't stand for it anymore." Faithful to Finch's instructions I stuck my head out of the window – holding the Web Ellis Trophy 25 floors above the traffic on the freeway below, pausing only to take another swig of the champers! The sound of the car horns was deafening – and feeding back through our open mics to blare out of speakers just seconds later in the same vehicles! After our Wallaby guests left at 10am we took a call from the Australian Rugby Union administration who told us the players had left the lid of the trophy behind, and we were asked to put it in a taxi. I'm sure the makers of this trophy could have never imagined the peril that awaited its arrival down under. Leaving nothing more to chance – I took the precious brass lid in my own car to the ARU's headquarters in North Sydney. I doubt whether this perpetual gong has been on a wilder ride since. These days only the hands of World Cup players are allow to touch this trophy and the idea that it could be held outside the top story window of a skyscraper would be unthinkable.

The football season of 1992 would coincide with the staging of the Barcelona Olympic Games, and a long coveted dream of covering the greatest show on earth was about to come true.

CHAPTER 9

BARCELONA

Every sports reporter wants to cover an Olympic Games. It's the Holy Grail. The greatest athletes, the biggest celebrities, the whole atmosphere is off the charts. And for me the 1992 Games were even more special. They were going to be held in Barcelona.

I wasn't a big traveller at that time. I'd only been to Europe once, about 10 years earlier. A mate and I had flown over to London, caught the train to Dover and hopped the ferry across the Channel to Calais then made our way to Barcelona. It was love at first sight. I was overwhelmed by Barcelona then and I'm still in awe of it now. I rated it ahead of New York, London and Paris as the world's best city. For some reason everything about Barcelona strikes a chord with me – the people, the food, the architecture – and when it was announced that the city had won the Olympic bid I had a visceral urge to start brushing-up on my limited Spanish.

At the time FM radio's version of '*where there's a will there's a way*' was translated to: '*where there's a sponsor – there's a plane ticket.*' If you could find someone or company to put up the cash you could go just about anywhere.

Triple M was only keen on the idea of covering the games 'as long as we don't have to pay for it.' The challenge of finding a sponsor wasn't daunting at all – but there was just one small hoop to jump through first. Accreditation.

You know when you watch the Olympics on TV and there's all these big plastic cards hanging around peoples' necks? That is their accreditation, and it is gold – and just as elusive. The big media

With Rugby tragic Mulray and Wallaby and Randwick legends Simon Poidevin, Mark Ella and Gary Ella at Coogee Oval after the Galloping Greens gave Bath a bath in the World Club Championship final.

organisations pay huge money to become rights holders and can command as many accreditations as they want. The non-rights holders like me have to stand in the queue and hope there are still some left by the time we get to the front of the line.

When I first contacted the Australian Olympic Committee about accreditation, I wasn't given a lot of hope. Once the big guns like Channel 7, the ABC, News Limited and Fairfax had got hold of all the passes they needed there wasn't going to be many left over and I was told I was way down the queue.

Then, as if I had been destined to go along, Triple M finance guy Peter Switzer said he knew someone who might be able to help – a surf club friend connected to someone high up at the AOC. Peter spoke to his mate, his mate spoke to his mate and his mate spoke to ... well, I don't know who he spoke to but I do know a couple of weeks later I had my accreditation. The day I opened that letter was one of the best of my life.

With the accreditation sorted getting a sponsor was not an issue. Our sales team made a few calls and an equipment hire company jumped onboard. One of the sales guys stuck his head around the corner and told me: “You’re going to Barcelona mate”. I couldn’t believe it. The first thing I did was go out and buy a flash new suit with the latest Euro cut. I didn’t realise a daily temperature of about 35 degrees would be awaiting me, and nor did I know the standard Olympic reporter’s uniform was t-shirt, shorts and comfortable joggers, but what the heck. The Black Rat always travels in style (minus the gold tooth!)

If you were ever going to cover just one Olympics, this was the one. It was being held in the hometown of Olympic boss Juan Antonio Samaranch and the Dream Team was going to be there, so you just knew this global sports extravaganza was going to be something out of the box.

The Dream Team had been put together for a number of reasons. The amateur-only US basketball team had been having a horror run since college students Michael Jordan and Patrick Ewing had led them to the gold medal in LA in 1988. In Seoul four years later, with Jordan and Ewing by then professional NBA stars and ineligible to compete, the fulltime State-funded athletes from Russia had won the gold after beating the fulltime State-funded athletes from Yugoslavia in the final. The clean-cut US college kids could only manage bronze which didn’t go down too well with the American public or the US government PR department for that matter. So the Yanks decide to give the sport a ‘proper gander’ and bring in the NBA superstars to show the eastern European countries a thing or two about baskets and balls.

The Olympics had started to lose their gloss a little after some debacles in Seoul. Canadian sprinter Ben Johnson had been busted for steroids after winning the 100m and American boxer Roy Jones Junior was robbed in the light-middleweight boxing final which he lost in the ultimate hometown decision after belting the tripe out of South Korean Park Si-hun. In another boxing final, spectators invaded the ring and beat up the Kiwi judge after the South Korean lost the decision.

On top of all that young people were starting to turn off and the Dream Team was designed to win back the youth audience. Why watch a bunch of amateur no-names running around when they could see some of the highest-profile athletes in the world playing in the NBA?

Acutely aware of the need to keep the self-appointed leaders of the free world happy, the IOC changed their rules in 1989 to allow professional basketballers to compete in Barcelona. And what a team the Yanks put together: Jordan, Magic Johnson, Larry Bird, Charles Barkley, Scottie Pippen, Karl Malone, David Robinson, Ewing ... it was like the NBA Hall of Fame on tour.

Apart from my compulsory non-negotiable attendance at Dream Team games my bucket list included seeing a game at Camp Nou, the home stadium of Barcelona FC. The Poms will tell you Wembley is the cathedral of football. I won't buy that for a second. As a lifetime football tragic it has always been Camp Nou and sitting in the packed stands and watching a game there would be a dream come true.

I didn't have to wait long for it to become a reality. The Barcelona Olympics officially opened on 25 July 1992 when Paralympic archer Antonio Rebollo shot a flaming arrow into the cauldron and hometown boy Juan Antonio Samaranch said, 'let the Games begin'. In fact, they had actually started one night earlier when Italy played USA at Camp Nou, and I was there. The Olympic football competition often starts a night or two before the Opening Ceremony because they have so many games to get through that they can't manage it in the two weeks of official competition.

Back in 1992 the Olympic football tournament was for Under-23 players and to be honest I didn't know too many of them apart from the Australians, but that didn't worry me. I was going to Camp Nou to be part of a jam-packed chanting, seething capacity crowd of 95,000. Well, maybe not quite that many. The official attendance was 14,000 which in a stadium the size of Camp Nou looked like a fly on an elephant's back and the atmosphere wasn't exactly what I'd expected after watching dozens of Barca v Real Madrid games at the ground on TV over the years.

It was still great though. I was staggered by the size of the place, and sitting high up in the stands felt like clinging to the side of a steep mountain. It was one of the most memorable games I ever saw but strangely I can't recall a lot about it. I do remember a journalist from Romania sat next to me and asked where I was from. When I told him Australia he became excited. Turned out he was a big rugby union fan and he just wanted to bang on about David Campese.

The next day I checked out the MPC – or Main Press Centre – for the first time. As I wasn't working for a rights holder, I didn't have the top-level accreditation. My relatively limited access got me into the venues to watch the events and I could go along to media conferences but I couldn't ask questions. In fact, I couldn't even take a tape recorder inside an Olympic venue.

There was a consolation though. Because I wasn't required to stay at the media village, an Orwellian complex of apartment buildings way out of the city and frankly too far from the action. Every morning the main media contingent would have to climb onto buses and be transported into town and every night, after working late at events and filing their stories, get back onto the buses for the long ride back to the village. Meanwhile Lord Muck here was checking into the Expo Hotel, a very nice four-star joint right next to Barcelona Sants railway station and a short stroll walk to the town centre.

Even the Main Press Centre was just a short cab ride from my hotel and I headed out there the morning after the Italy–USA football game.

It was housed in these spectacular buildings designed for the Barcelona Exposition in 1929. They ran along the long Avenue of the Americas, coming off a huge circular intersection with a big fountain in the middle, called the Plaça d'Espanya. There were statues and columns and meticulously manicured shrubs and gardens everywhere. Once you got past the exposition buildings stairs and escalators led to the top of Montjuïc, a giant hill with spectacular views over the city and the setting for the Olympic stadium and swimming pool stood. It was mind-blowing.

The inside of the enormous MPC was just as impressive, accommodating 11,000 accredited media. The rights holders had their own offices with their names on the doors, like the *New York Times*, Reuters, Associated Press and News Limited but the non-rights holders, like me, got to sit and work in a vast open area, not far off the size of two football fields, with long bench tables and chairs. There were no designated areas, journos just lobbed wherever they could find a space and got to work. Overhead there were huge TV screens, live streaming from every venue. With so many events on at once it meant that the non-rights holders could cover everything without ever leaving that room if they wanted, and plenty did. Everything they needed was right there. You didn't even have to go outside for food. The MPC had bars, cafés – even McDonalds. If you wanted pizza you could get it delivered by good sorts on roller skates.

Given the rapid of evolution of digital technology since 1992, the facilities available at the Barcelona Olympics seemed pretty primitive by today's standards but for the time they were cutting edge. All accredited media were given what looked like a credit card and a pin number. There was no internet or mobile phones back then so to send stories to their offices in their home counties the journos had to use the phone lines. The phones in all the venues and the press centre had a system for reporters to swipe the card, punch in an individual code and attach their computer to the phone to send. At the end of the Games the media companies would get a bill for the amount of time their staff had spent on the line.

I was different, filing radio reports live to air twice a day either from my hotel room or reverse charges from a public phone. When I needed to send a recorded interview into my report I just put the receiver next to the tape recorder and pushed 'play'. As long as I was near a phone at the exact time the newsroom back in Sydney was expecting my call I was fine, so my visits to the MPC were few and far between.

But this day was different. There was no way any accredited journalist in Barcelona would miss out on what was happening at the MPC that morning: the Dream Team media conference.

It was the hottest ticket in town. Everywhere you looked around Barcelona there were reminders that the NBA stars were coming – the most obvious – a banner showing Michael Jordan in action that took up the wall of a ten-storey building. As well as the work areas, the MPC had about a dozen rooms set up for media conferences of different sizes, from an intimate 15–20-seater right up to a massive auditorium with a stage that seated about 1200. Needless to say that's where they held the Dream Team event and still wasn't big enough. It was standing room only.

I arrived early to secure a seat – as did the rest of the Aussie media contingent because there was a big news story bubbling away that involved the Australian team.

Nine months earlier in November 1991 the LA Lakers champion point guard Magic Johnson had announced that he was retiring after testing positive to HIV. It was huge at the time. Not a lot was known about the virus and many people mistakenly thought Johnson had AIDS and wouldn't survive much longer. In fact, he is still going strong today and such was his popularity that his fans simply wouldn't let him retire. Although he wasn't playing professionally at the time, in February 1992 he was voted by the public to take part in the NBA All-Star Game in Orlando, Florida. When he got through that without any problems – he actually top scored, sank the winning three-pointer and was voted MVP – it was enough to have him selected for the Dream Team. Everyone in the world was excited to have him taking part in the Olympics.

Well, maybe not everyone.

In the lead-up to the Games Australian captain Phil Smyth said he would only play against the Dream Team if Johnson had received a medical clearance beforehand and Boomers player Ray Borner said he would refuse to play against the US if Johnson was in the team. Another Aussie, Mark Bradtke, said he felt that all players in the tournament should be tested for HIV before being cleared to play.

Even though there was no certainty that Australia would even play the Americans at the Games – and as it turned out they didn't – it created a furore and the hottest angle for the Australian reporters. Nobody else seemed to give a damn. They were just excited to see the NBA superstars in the flesh. You knew that this was no ordinary media conference when some of the press started applauding as the Dream Team walked out onto the stage led by coach Chuck Daly. In media circles the biggest insult you can give a sportswriter is to call them a 'fan'. In that auditorium that day there were about 1000 of them.

It didn't take long to realise much of the US media wasn't really interested in reporting what the Dream Team had to say. They just wanted the bragging rights of telling mates back home they had asked Michael Jordan or Magic Johnson a question. Some of the others just had no idea.

Anyone wanting to ask a question had to get in a line down the middle of the auditorium. When they got to the end of the line they'd be handed a microphone, say where they were from and direct their question to the player of choice. When the system was explained there was a mad scramble as about a hundred ran to get to the front of the line. There wasn't any point in me lining up as I didn't have the right accreditation, but a Channel 7 TV reporter asked Magic Johnson the question that all the Aussie media wanted answered: how did he feel about the comments by Phil Smyth and the other Boomers?

Magic's answered: "It doesn't make any difference to me if they let me play against them or not. We'll beat them with me or without me."

The players were also quizzed on why they were staying in a luxury villa on the outskirts of town and not the athletes' village like everyone else. Chuck Daly answered by asking Patrick Ewing and David Robinson to stand up. They were both over 7 foot tall and most of the others in the team weren't far behind them.

"Can you find me a bed to fit these guys at the athletes' village?" Daly asked, but that wasn't the only reason. Later that day the Dream Team went out to visit the village and they were swamped by athletes from all over the world wanting autographs and pictures. Residency in the village would not have afforded them a moment's peace.

The question about the Dream's team's exclusive digs and a few more from the Australians about Magic Johnson were the only sensible ones all day. Some of the more unbelievable questions included one from a Japanese woman asking Michael Jordan why his team had so many black players. A Norwegian journo was curious to know why they scored two points for a goal in basketball.

"In football it is one point for a goal," he said. "So why in basketball is it two points?"

Karl gave it his best shot, explaining how basketball had been invented in America by Dr Naismith and when he worked out the scoring system he had come up with two points for a field goal.

"He just said two points for a field goal. Two points for a field goal and one point from the free throw line and three points from outside ..."

The reporter wasn't satisfied.

"But why two points?"

Big Karl finally snapped.

"Hell, I don't know. That's just the way it is. You gotta get with the programme son. You're not in Norway now." The Oslo drongo finally gave-up.

I guess you could forgive the ignorance and curiosity of foreign media not engaged with basketball as a national past time but some of the Americans had no excuses. One guy stood in the line for about half an hour and when he finally got to ask Michael Jordan who was winning all the money when the players were betting on golf.

"Me," said Jordan, and the reporter went back to his seat.

Larry Bird summed it up when another US reporter asked him how he was enjoying the Olympics.

"Well," said Bird. "It was fine until I had to come in here and listen to all this BS."

It soon became obvious that Charles Barkley was the star of the show – on and off the court. He ended up being the highest point scorer of the tournament but he was just as good with a microphone in his hand. He knew what made a good headline. He oozed menace and charisma.

When asked what he knew about USA's first opponent Angola, he answered: "All I know about Angola is that Angola is in trouble."

Questioned about walking the streets of Barcelona at night without bodyguards he held up his fists and said, "These are my bodyguards." He was hilarious.

That night was the Opening Ceremony and the next day the Games started in earnest. In the morning I watched Kathy Watt won Australia's first gold medal in the cycling road race. In the afternoon I went to watch the Dream Team's first game at Badalona, about 20 kilometres northeast of the Barcelona CBD, and Charles Barkley was right. Angola was in a lot of trouble. One thing I'll never forget was what happened at the tip-off. Everyone had their cameras ready to get the ultimate 'I was there when...' shot and when the ball went up all the flashes went off at once. It was like a bolt of lightning had hit the stadium.

The Americans won 116–48 but the game wasn't a complete write-off for the Angolans. Not all of them anyway. I remember seeing that one of the players had given his camera to a team-mate who was sitting on the bench. This guy was marking Michael Jordan and when they were near the bench he kept calling out to his mate to take a picture.

The Dream Team game started at 4.30pm and when it finished I had about an hour to get to the Australia vs Ghana soccer game at a place called Sabadell, another 15 kilometres north west. There was no media bus going from the basketball to the football stadium but my accreditation pass gave me free public transport and I decided to catch a train. What could possibly go wrong? Plenty as it turned out.

You know that Steve Martin stand-up routine where he talks about the difficulty of getting around in France and he says, "it's like those French have a different word for *everything*."

Well, it's the same in Spain. You might think little separates the Spanish and English languages. Think again. They have virtually nothing in common and the further you drift from the tourist spots of Barcelona, the more evident the language barrier becomes. Unfortunately, my grasp of Spanish is rather limited. I know '*Hola*' which means 'hello', '*Si*' which means 'yes', '*cerveza*' which means 'beer' and '*Adios amigo*' which, of course means 'adios amigo', but put me on a train trying to work out which station from which to alight and I'm in a lot of trouble.

The problem was that Sabadell is a big place – the fifth largest city in Spain. I didn't know which station was close to the football stadium and I couldn't get through to the other passengers to help me. I eventually resorted to sign language. I was pointing to the accreditation pass hanging around my neck, pretending to kick and head a football, and as much as they seemed to find me very amusing the Spaniards had no idea what I was going on about. With the 7pm kick-off getting ever closer I took a gamble and jumped off at the next station, hoping for the best. I figured upon exiting the station I would be in the middle of a bustling city centre with buses, cabs and plenty of English-speaking Olympic officials milling around to help me on my way.

Not quite. It was like that scene in *Butch Cassidy and The Sundance Kid* where Butch has talked Sundance into moving to Bolivia. They get off the train and there is nothing there except empty streets and a guy walking past with a lama. I didn't even have the guy with the lama. The streets were completely deserted.

By now I was starting to get a little worried. The time was ticking away and not only did I have no idea how to get to Sabatell's Estadi Municipal de la Nova Creu Alta where the game was being played, I couldn't even pronounce it. With no alternative, I started walking and then the gods of Olympia smiled on me. Out of nowhere came a cab. An empty cab. I started shouting and waving and the driver pulled over. I ran across, jumped in and with a combination of pidgin Spanish ('Olympica futabola, si, si?') and showing him the name of the stadium in my media handbook, somehow made him understand where I was headed. He gave me the thumbs-up, stuck a tape of Gipsy Kings into his cassette player, cranked it up to full volume and got me to the game with seconds to spare.

After all the trouble of getting there I hoped for a sparkling start to the Socceroos' Olympic campaign but Ghana had other plans. They were really giving it to our players, and the Ghanaian spectators were returning serve to any Australians within earshot.

Just six months earlier the biggest boxing match in Australian history had taken place in Melbourne when almost 40,000 people had watched local hero Jeff Fenech take on Ghana's world champion Azumah Nelson at Princes Park. The year before Jeff had fought Nelson in Las Vegas and was robbed by the judges who scored it a draw when Stevie Wonder could have seen Jeff had won hands down. The rematch in Melbourne was seen as Jeff's chance to right the wrong and the Aussie press had given it to Nelson from the moment he arrived in the country. Unfortunately for Jeff and his many fans things didn't go to script, with Nelson bashing him up for eight rounds before the referee stopped the fight to save him further punishment.

A similar fate was awaiting the Socceroos at Sabatell and the Ghanaian fans were letting us know it. When the score was 2–0 one of them turned to me and said: “Hey, you Australians are losing everything these days”. In the second half Mark Viduka scored to bring it back to 2–1 and our boys seemed to be mounting a late charge, at which point the Ghanaians in the crowd started up a chant: ‘Fuck you Aus-tray-lia, fuck you Aus-tray-lia’.

It finished 3–1 and I would have loved to get straight out of there and head back to Barcelona but once again it wasn’t that simple. The press guys had to wait around for both team media conferences, then write and file their stories and the media bus wasn’t going to leave until they were all finished. By the time all the interviews were over, and the journos got into the work room it was pretty late. One guy wrote his story, plugged his computer into the phone, pushed ‘send’ and ... nothing happened. He tried again and got the same lack of response, so he called over one of the Olympic liaison people who looked blankly and made a phone call. About 15 minutes later the local telephone company technician arrived – dressed in his pyjamas, dressing gown and slippers. He got under the desk, fiddled around with some wires, fixed the problem, and went back to bed. The guy filed and we finally all jumped on the bus for the hour-long trip back to the MPC in Barcelona, which would have been fine if it wasn’t getting scarily close to the time when I had to do my live radio cross to the studio in Sydney.

With about 10 minutes left the bus had hit the outskirts of the city and if I could get off and run to my hotel I could just make it in time. I went up to the driver and asked him to let me off. He shook his head and pointed straight ahead.

‘MPC,’ he said.

I told him I had to get to a phone so I could file.

‘MPC,’ he said.

‘Radio, radio,’ I said reverting to the hand signals and pretending to talk into a microphone.

He kept shaking his head and pointing.

'MPC.'

By now I'm sweating bullets. My career is flashing before my eyes. I'm desperate. I've got to get off that bus and get to a phone. I do what any self-respecting sports reporter would do in such a situation. I reach into my wallet, pull out a handful of local currency and wave it under his nose.

He just keeps shaking his head.

'MPC.'

And then it dawns on me. Anyone who has ever been to an Olympic Games will know that there is something that Olympic tragics value a lot more than mere cash. Pins.

Yeah, I know, it sounds ridiculous but that's the way it is every four years. The first time I saw people swapping lapel pins in Barcelona I had no idea what was going on. They lay out blankets on footpaths and spread out all their little commemorative pins which might have sponsors logos on them or mark the days until the Games start or, most valuable of all, commemorate Opening and Closing ceremonies. Dozens of people mill around all day, bartering and swapping their pins. As long as they have the Olympic rings on them, people want them. In Barcelona everywhere you went people would ask you for one. Whether it was the waitress bringing you your breakfast, the volunteer checking you through security at a venue or just a stranger in a bar, you'd hear it a hundred times a day.

'Peen?'

When we arrived at Barcelona and presented our accreditation at the MPC greeting desk for the first time we were given a welcome kit that contained things like a media guide, maps of the city, vouchers for free Coke and McDonalds, a watch which stopped working after two hours and about half a dozen pins in the shape of the Games mascot Cobi, a sheepdog in the style of a Picasso painting.

Luckily, I had a couple of them in my pocket.

'Peen?' I said to the driver pulling them out.

He jumped on the brakes and within minutes I was in my room delivering my report. Given everything that had happened to me during the day and what I had to go through to provide our listeners with my first-hand, on-the-spot commentary I was feeling pretty pleased with myself when I signed off with, 'Frank Vincent reporting live from Barcelona'. I sat back waiting for the news director to tell me what a brilliant job I had done, what an asset I was to the organisation and how there would be a little something extra in my pay packet for the month.

Not so much.

'Why didn't you get an interview with Kathy Watt?' he said.

And that was the end of day one.

The next 14 days were more of the same. It was like being in some kind of surreal fantasy bubble although maybe that had something to do with the arrival of my 'assistant' Lou Dimovitch. Lou was a journalist who worked with me at Triple M. Before I left for Barcelona I told him he should come over and sleep on my floor and help me out with my work. After a few days covering the Games I'd rung him to say how great it was so he thought, 'what the hell' took a couple of weeks off and headed over. The idea was he'd help me score interviews but I had another score in mind. The first night he said, 'is there anything I can do for you?' I told him I was dying for a smoke and pointed him in the direction of Las Ramblas – or The Rambler as the Aussie tourists called it.

Las Ramblas is a long street that goes from the city to the harbour and it's where the night-time action really takes place in Barcelona.

There's bars, nightclubs, street-stalls, hookers, dealers and anything else you can think of. One of the great things about Barcelona is that it is a city that really comes to life at night. Maybe it's because they have a siesta in the middle of the day, but they like to stay up late. It came as a bit of a shock to be in a cab or bus rolling through the streets after covering a night-time event and seeing families with their little kids in flood-lit playgrounds at 10.30pm. The playground for the big kids was Las Ramblas.

When Lou got there the first young bloke who asked if he needed anything took his money and disappeared never to be seen again. The second attempt was more successful and Lou arrived back at the hotel with some hash which we proceeded to knock off in my room. I'm not a big fan of hash, I find it hurts my throat, but I managed to struggle through.

Apart from that, Lou's major contribution was to bring back to Australia all the big books of statistics I picked up at the MPC. They were put out by all the different international sporting associations and for some reason I thought stats like the Ukrainian Under-16 boys' long jump record would be vitally important for the rest of my career. Maybe it was the after-effects of the hash. Anyway, there were too many of them to fit into my suitcase so Lou brought them back for me and I finally got my hands on them about 10 years later.

I'm not sure what Lou did while I was out working because he didn't have any accreditation but I'm pretty sure he was having a good time. I know I was. Just being over there during the Games was incredible. I went along to all the Dream Team pool matches and as many of the Australian events as I could. The only problem was not being able to interview anyone in the Games venues but I got around that in two ways. First, I'd done as many interviews with Aussie athletes as I could before I even left Australia. I'd got them on tape, coded and labelled them and left them with the news room. That way when I mentioned them in one of my reports I could tell the producers which tape to grab and they could insert the recording into the right spot. The other way was to arrange to speak to athletes outside the venues. I'd go along to training sessions or media conferences and ask them if they'd meet me at another time. Some of them, like sprinter Melinda Gainsford and swimmers Kieren Perkins and his main 1500m freestyle rival Glen Housman were great. I'd make a time to meet them outside the athletes' village and they'd come out and have a chat. Another one was Socceroo star Ned Zelic. Ned was the next big thing in Australian football at the time. He'd just signed to join the giant German club Borussia Dortmund after the Games which was a major deal for a 21-year-old from Canberra. I remember when Australia played Mexico all these Borussia Dortmund fans came along to cheer him on. Ned was so good to me. He actually came in to my hotel for an interview. Someone else I saw at my hotel but I didn't have the heart to disturb was Australian marathon runner Lisa Ondieki. She and her husband, Kenyan runner Yobes Ondieki, were having breakfast at the table next to me the morning after her race. She had gone into the marathon as one of the favourites but was one of plenty of runners who couldn't finish. The race had started at 6.30pm because of concerns about the heat in the middle of the day but it was still an estimated 96 degrees Fahrenheit or 35.5 Celsius when the runners were on the course. One of them ended up in hospital and I reckon Lisa couldn't have been far off it. I've never seen anyone look worse than she did at breakfast that morning.

One incredible interview I did get was with 'athlete of the century' Carl Lewis. Carl was the reigning Olympic 100m champion following the disqualification of Ben Johnson in Seoul but had failed to qualify for the US team for Barcelona so was over there representing his sponsors. That meant his media conference wasn't in an official Olympic venue and I could go along with my trusty tape recorder. I grabbed him after the main part of the function and he couldn't have been more generous with his time. That's how it was over there. You just didn't know who you'd see or bump into. You'd go along to the swimming and see Greg Norman or Michael Douglas or Evander Holyfield in the stands. Arnold Schwarzenegger was over there as health and fitness ambassador for President George Bush Snr but took time out to open Planet Hollywood Barcelona.

We all turned up thinking we'd be enjoying free drinks and food with Arnie in the bar of the newest branch of the restaurant chain he owned with Bruce Willis and Sylvester Stallone but it turned out to be just a big hole in the ground. Arnie told us it was where the restaurant was going to be once they built it, and then called for questions. One thing I learnt that day was that it isn't just American journalists who ask stupid questions when they're face to face with their idols. There was a reporter who asked a long question in German that was every bit as inconsequential as anything that was asked of the Dream Team.

Arnie translated. 'This gentleman has asked me what my favourite food is,' he said, 'It's strudel.'

I must admit I didn't pass that scoop on to my listeners, but there was plenty of other news that I did send back in my reports. The things I saw and the people I interviewed were just amazing. It was without doubt one of the major highlights of my career – and my life.

When it was all over I had to have a break so I had arranged to take a few days off on the way home. I'd got to know the Sydney representative for the company that handled publicity for the Plaza

Hotel in New York. The Plaza is best known to Australians as the luxury hotel opposite Central Park where Paul Hogan stayed in *Crocodile Dundee* and back in 1992 it was owned by none other than Donald Trump. I asked my contact if she could get me a good rate and she did better than that. She arranged four nights free of charge. I had a great stay there. I must remember to thank The Donald next time I see him.

Relaxed, refreshed and ready to bask in the glory of my successful foreign assignment, I headed to the airport for the trip back to Sydney and the continuation of my blissfully happy partnership with my own cheer squad – the entire Mulray Bunch at Triple M. Before I got on my flight I called my mother to give her my flight details and ask her to pick me up and give me a lift home when I landed.

'Sure,' she said. 'Oh, have you heard the news?' Doug Mulray has resigned. There's a new morning show. Someone called Club Veg.'

I nearly dropped the phone. I knew Club Veg, a couple of guys named Malcolm Lees and Vic Davies who had been doing the afternoon shift, had no interest in sport on their show. The closest they came was comedy spots by their writer Steve Quinn who did a Scottish character named Wee Dougie McCrutchnut who would occasionally take the piss out of sport. I fumed all the way back to Australia. When I got in the car with my mother she had the radio tuned to Triple M.

The first thing I heard was an ad for Club Veg and a voice-over saying: 'And don't forget to buy your Wee Dougie McCrutchnut T-shirt.' I started screaming.

'You've gotta be kidding me. He's got his own fucking t-shirt?'

I knew then the Games were well and truly over. The Black Rat was about to start a whole new chapter.

CHAPTER 10

A NEW CHAPTER

Most of us are familiar with a sixth sense, a subliminal belief that something beyond the obvious is afoot and somehow our awareness of it provides no power in controlling the planets as they realign.

Such was the case in the dying days of my career at Triple M.

Working in such a coveted job carries the inevitability of jealousy, bitterness, resentment – and that's just when you're dealing with some colleagues. Outside the work place you know there's a queue of hopefuls extending to the Queensland border. As someone who stood in that very line, I know exactly what pressures are brought to bear on those lucky enough to be on 'the inside' and how hard they fight to stay there.

After returning from what I at least thought was a triumphant self-financed tour of Barcelona I became aware that my proactivity and passion was amounting to nothing for those who had me squarely in their cross hairs. A Gold Medal for effort at the games was the last thing my nemesis in management had in mind. Like a sniper licking his lips my executioner had been waiting for my most powerful ally Doug Mulray to leave before pulling the trigger in a new and novel version of 'rat' extermination. The Black Rat was a goner.

The downside of being on the Mulray Bunch would indeed prove to be my dispensability once Mullos had pulled the pin. But while I was very much alive to the threat, I clung to a hope that my talents and potential would be recognised in their own right. I had after all proven to be versatile. I could pull any shift at a moment's notice and hoped memories of how I once salvaged the Mulray show itself would remain fresh in the minds of the very same bosses, who gushed at the time and now rushed to usher me out the door.

My career was back on track after the Triple M treachery, thanks to 2Day FM program director Brad March.

Not once did I stop to contemplate my cockiness – a necessary part of the job for many reasons – was now being conveniently perceived as the 'over confidence' of someone who simply cruised in the slip stream of a superstar. I thought my ability was worthy of a glowing appraisal without any flattery from the ambient glow of the molten red Mulray machine. But I would be proven wrong, and in the end, it became easy for me to be painted as the architect of my own demise.

In the end, the sword onto which I would impale myself happened in the form of every breakfast shift worker's worst nightmare – a sleep in. I had spent the previous evening working at the annual Rugby league awards night then known as the Rothmans Medal, the precursor to what's now known as the Dally M Awards before the prohibition of advertising and sponsorships by tobacco companies. On this disastrous morning I was indeed reaching for a smoke, and not necessarily of the packaged variety, after listening to an answering machine message from the Triple M program director for me to come in and 'discuss my future' with him and the boss of news at the time. I knew it was curtains. I didn't phone back and nor did I present myself physically before the firing squad.

My first impulse was to seek Doug's counsel on the phone. He had saved my skin so many times before but this time he was gone and put it to me bluntly after I entertained the notion of some influence that may have lingered after his exit. "Frank – I'm afraid there is nothing I can do for you." I was gone by the end of that day, No goodbyes, no farewell, no best wishes. Feel free to cry right here.

Brad March, 2Day FM Program Director.

Ten years of my life had come a halt every bit as abrupt as the encounter between a speeding train and a brick wall. I recalled my disappointment of never getting a chance to broadcast some great interviews from the Rothmans Medal, but as I snored away in an alcohol induced stupor the material was destined never to be heard again. I didn't have the same fate in mind for myself and within days my great mate Paul Holmes was phoning to tell me his employer 2Day FM wanted to hear my reel. It turned out to be a lifeline from the heavens.

It didn't take long to be pulling the odd casual shift at the old enemy, before being enlisted to work as a roving reporter for the *Wendy Harmer Show*, taking to the streets to shirtfront punters on the issues of the day with what had become my customary cheekiness.

My career had been salvaged. Thank you, Brad March, for believing in me. I love you brother. I had taken a serious 'haircut' as they say in the business, earning less than half of my Triple M wage, but more valuable than any salary was the rescue of my career, and a perception from the outside at least that I had simply switched camps after Doug's departure. Only one radio executive had a sniff of the actual circumstances. When my bell was tolling, I had exploratory discussions about jumping back onto the AM band with 2UW program director Cherie Romero. After hearing I had left Triple M she challenged me on whether I had approached her to in an attempt to 'jump before I was pushed.' The instincts from this seasoned radio operator were impeccable as it turned out but to her credit Cherie never made her suspicions the subject of any sinister 'broadcast.' It was in the vault.

Back in the saddle at 2DayFM, recording an advertisement.

In this game reputation is everything. To be bobbing up on 2DayFM so soon after leaving Triple M was arguably the luckiest break of my career until then. I had ducked an 'Exocet missile' – and absorbed a sobering reality check at the same time. If in fact I had been starting to take things for granted every ounce of that complacency had been shaken out of me by my brutal and unceremonious disposal from Bondi Junction. They stopped just short of throwing me from the 25th floor window, but somehow, I had still been feeling the impact of a faceplant on the concrete below.

My sneaking suspicions of an ugly end at the Ms – a place I considered to be a second family home – had manifested just as I feared, but suddenly I was bouncing back. 2DayFM turned out to be this stuntman's pile of cardboard boxes on the ground below, and I'll forever be in the debt of my best mate Holmsey. But the savage finale notwithstanding I manage until this day to retain the fondest memories of my Triple M Days – my first crack at the serious big time. I'm proud to have been a part of what history now judges as breakthrough radio, and it's nothing other than a privilege to have been among the ranks of genuine pioneers.

Many of the original Triple M crew had a terrific reunion in late 2022 and it we all picked up where we left off like it was yesterday. Doug was there – and for once he seemed human, just like the rest of us! His wit was as sharp as ever, but somehow the humility delivering by his advancing years had ensured he was one of us after all.

The reunion at The Oakes Hotel was a real sentimental romp, organised by former jocks Trevor Jackson and Sue Moses.

It was sensational to catch up with Rob Duckworth, Ian Rogerson, Dave Gibson, Michael Andersen, Dave Carlson, Barbara Wilton, Rod Muir, Gavin Morris, Reggea Ellis, Richard Clapton (*still* a committed fan!), Tim Webster, Peter Switzer, Mike Drayson and Tim Sheridan.

One of the smoothest voices in the business and former Triple M floater Pete Armstrong recited a special letter from listener called 'The Last Frontier'. The fax read like this:

"Where do the wild men walk in Sydney radio? Where do you look for the real characters? The living legends and folk heroes of the industry? Hidden behind all the neat office fronts, is there somewhere? A last frontier where you can find the kind of characters who burst through bar room doors with a gun swinging on each hip? Who work hard, died hard and play hard. Or, the other way round. You won't find them at 2DAY FM, 2UW or 2GB. Where are the undisciplined, the unruly, the untamed, the masters of the long lunch, the employees of any other radio station who were bound to be fired? But you can't fire these because you need them. Why? Triple M, where else?"

Widely known as the 'father of FM radio in Australia' Rod Muir also addressed the gathering of those who were only there – and knew each other – because of his vision.

"We had some enormous times. And there is a truism on radio that what you find you get in the corridor, is the message that goes up the stick. You can tell a number one station just by walking through the corridor. We had that freshness."

Doug then paid tribute to Rod.

"There would be no Triple M without that man there. He lobbied for a thing (FM radio) that we should have had 20 years before."

"We were the right thing, at the right time, in the right place, with the right attitude. It was just an astounding thing to be a part of...we were blessed to have that thing."

"The mood in the joint, and the mood on the street told you when it was."

"It was a joy to be there."

"When I left radio, I was over it. I wanted the privacy. And I kind of distanced myself that I ever did that (Triple M breakfast show). It was kind of like a fantasy.

"It always felt good to be with you guys. Be together. And, I want to thank you for that. Thank you."

The room then honoured the memories of deceased on air colleagues in a tribute titled 'The Fallen Friends Of The Ms':

Jono Coleman, Sammy Power, Stuart Cranney, Ken Sterling, Warwick 'Wazza The Rock Dog' Rankin, Jon 'Ratso' Kennedy and Vic Davies and Lou Dimovitch.

"They were amazing people. And they were part of our extended family," Trevor Jackson told the gathering.

"Their spirit lives on."

I was very saddened to learn Lou Dimovitch had passed just weeks before the reunion. We were good buddies, who shared a wonderful understanding of each other. We were always on the same page. We loved the same music and an appreciation for the more subtle things in life. As a journalist Lou guided on newsworthiness, scripting and delivery. We also had in common a love of motor racing, and he would eventually work as a producer on the Australian franchise of Top Gear. He had a distinguished production career spanning more than 30 years, producing documentaries, news, sport, travel, entertainment and lifestyle programs in roles with Network Ten, Channel Nine, SBS and Foxtel. Go well Lou.

Reuniting with my hero Doug at the Triple reunion, just months before he passed.

I know he would have loved the Triple M reunion, and the chance to catch-up with colleagues from when it all began for him in Sydney after growing up in Port Kembla. He featured in many of the stories swapped all night. As you can imagine those paid to talk for a living were never going to be short of a word.

Little could many of us at the reunion suspect that November 4, 2022 would be Doug's last goodbye. Five months later he would be signing off for the last time, surrounded by loved ones after succumbing to liver disease.

The world of Sydney radio was rocked by Doug's passing at the age of 71, and the tributes flowed, led by close friend and former Triple M colleague Andrew 'The Boy Genius' Denton, who said working with Mullos was like "being on a rollercoaster – but hanging on from the outside – and sometimes from underneath".

"He had a perfect radio voice... Doug was a brilliant, spontaneous broadcaster," Denton said, adding his collaboration with Doug was "one of the great creative partnerships of my life and my career".

"Doug Mulray made himself a legend on Double J back in the day, the sort of counter culture ABC youth network. He was crazy... but he was much more than crazy,"

"He started at Triple M when Triple M started. So he was part of the birth of FM radio in Australia. Within a decade he had taken Triple M to the top of radio, top of all radio in Sydney. And the reason was, he was crazy. He had a genius for radio.... Doug was absolutely suited to radio and he could do it all. He could do brilliant impersonations. He was so fast. He could perform. He could sing. And he was prepared to try anything. So, in the years when I was working with him, we had an audience of about 1 million, and it was everything from barristers to garbos listening

With my good mate Pete 'The Casual One' Armstrong, the most talented floating announcer in the country with inimitable golden tones.

in.... He was just funny in a way you could never predict."

"Dougy, he was a very self-lacerating man. He never thought he was good enough, bit I think he knew at the end of his life he'd done something which is given to very few – he had brought genuine joy to so many people's lives, and that's what he brought into mine."

21 century Triple M Sydney breakfast host, Mick Molloy, described Doug's breakfast romp as "the greatest show in radio at the time – and possibly ever."

"Any of us who work in radio owe him a huge debt....he was a trailblazer, a pioneer, a maverick, all of the above. He should have some kind of Triple M Mount Rushmore or a big statue out the front."

Molloy struggled to hide his emotions in a moving on-air tribute to the Great Man.

"It is a terrible morning. A huge gaping hole has been left in the landscape of FM radio, particularly in Sydney where Doug Mulray ruled since 1982. He was the man, he was a legendary radio performer. For anyone in comedy, particularly going into radio, he was considered the biggest star in the firmament. He ruled Sydney radio for a long time.

"A lot of us who do this for a job owe him a great debt. He paved the way in many ways. He was like a god on the FM train, he worked at the station and just dominated it. He transformed Triple M Sydney, and his impact reverberated around Australia. This is an important passing, especially for people in our industry."

2GB breakfast host Ben Fordham said: "If there's a radio station in heaven, they better get the dump button ready, because Doug Mulray is coming."

Southern Cross Austereo CEO Grant Blackley said Doug was "radio royalty and an absolute legend."

"He was instrumental in changing the face of radio on Triple M and became a household name. He was deeply opinionated, highly intelligent and one very cheeky bugger."

"Thank you, Dougie, for entertaining us and ensuring we never took life too seriously. We will miss you. Vale Doug Mulray."

One of Mulray's chart classics – *You Are Soul* – dominated the airwaves on the morning of his passing, and as glowing obituaries continued an anonymous listener summed Doug up as succinctly as anyone, calling Triple M to say: "He didn't push the boundaries of radio, he blew them up!"

The Project's Lisa Wilkinson reflected warmly on her days of working alongside Doug at Channel 10, describing Doug as "this beautiful man... a comic genius, breakfast radio icon, host of TV's *Beauty & The Beast*, and one of the kindest, most generous souls I've ever been lucky enough to work with." Wow.

I was interviewed by Sky News to pay my own tribute, reliving those amazing days with Doug in the Mulray Bunch, and recalling our free seafood breakfast delivered by a wonderful German man Doug referred to as 'Hans the former U Boat Commander.'

Consistent with his famously generous spirit Doug was actually going to write the foreword for this book, but as he fought his illness the lovely Alison Drower offered to take up the task.

I was particularly fond of my catch-up with Alison Drower at the Triple M reunion. She is a wonderful woman who went on from the Ms newsroom to become heavily involved in the coverage of motorsports – just as I did at Channel 10 after we had both made our names at a rock 'n' roll station. But Alison was putting an extra laying of icing on her career cake by joining my dear friend Richard Wilkins as co-host of the Australian MTV franchise. Richard too has always been a great supporter of mine, since the day he laughed as

I trotted out Whitey's "the smell of liniment is imminent line" at a Rugby League grand final. From that day onwards he stopped calling me 'mate' and addressed me as Frank. Richard was always superbly presented, and when I questioned him once on his unfaltering sartorial style he said: "Frank, you just never know when someone is going to shove a camera in your face."

Simply put Richard Wilkins is a class act, and way beyond his broadcasting talents a Master of Ceremonies par excellence. He was so adaptable, quick to absorb information at any notice and articulate it seamlessly. His public presentations at events from fashion shows, music nights to football games and first night premieres were always polished and executed with aplomb. He had a big brain to go with his slick image, and he was the gentlest of men, always ready to oblige with friendly advice. It was always a great pleasure to catch-up with Richard at Red Carpet events and opening night parties.

Richard taught me a lot about the importance of thinking on your feet – literally. It's one thing to *sit* behind a radio panel and chat away but it's a whole new level when rising to speak before an audience in large public spaces. Thanks to Richard I could learn from an absolute master. I was relying upon every inch of the Wilkins' example at a Bondi Junction shopping centre after joining 2DayFM and enlisted to compere proceedings for the launch of a new health and fitness video by supermodel Claudia Schiffer.

Initially the promoters wanted me to donate my services in exchange for mere thrill of being in the presence of the German beauty. I hit back by quoting one of Claudia's runway colleagues Linda Evangelista, in telling the organisers "I don't get out of bed for less than $800 bucks a day." (Way short of Evangelista's $10,000 demand I hasten to add.) So, after behaving like it was their own coin, the promoters finally coughed up to guarantee I had more than an instant infatuation with a Goddess to show for my time.

Looking back, maybe I should have been paying her to be in the company of such a stunning, delightful, classy human being. She was drop dead gorgeous but very humble, and politely declined my offer to interview her as she signed autographs for a long line of starstruck shoppers. So being the frustrated commentator I've always been I decided to 'call' the signing of her signature. "Now ladies and gentlemen, there's a big looping C, followed by a rather tidy L..." and on it went. She had clearly never encountered such Australian humour and returned after the signing to thank me personally.

Weak in the presence of world class beauty, hosting the Sydney launch of a health and wellbeing video produced by supermodel Claudia Schiffer.

It was the dizziest of heights when Claudia leaned towards me, close to my face to say: "You were great today. You were very funny," It was almost whispered in her inimitable sultry way. Infatuation suddenly ballooned into full blown love! Smitten doesn't quite cut it! Claudia was at the height of her fame, featuring that year in one of the many *Vogue* cover appearances in her career. But once again I was encountering a mega celebrity with a lovely nature that defied the demeanour one might expect from one of the best known faces on the planet.

It was great to be joining 2Day FM at a time when the perennial bridesmaid of Sydney FM radio was finally on the brink of toppling the once mighty Ms. It wasn't a case of 'the emperor has no clothes' at Bondi Junction. They had no emperor! Doug's abdication as the King of the Corny Flakes paved the way in yellow bricks for the emerging queen of the same breakfast slot – Wendy Harmer.

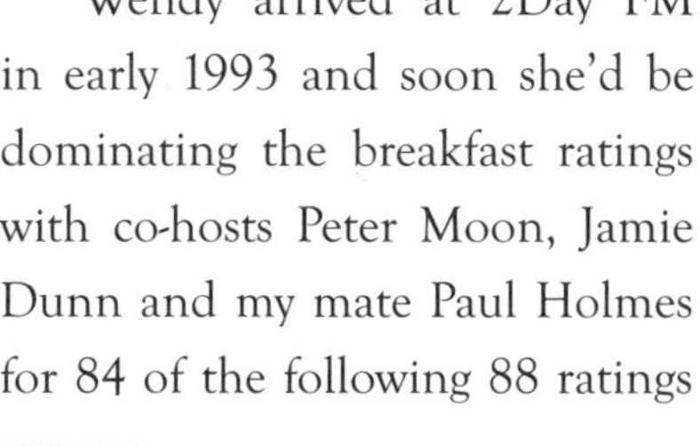

My career was hanging in the balance before I was thrown a rope by 2Day FM — but there was a catch — I had to climb down the side of skyscraper as stunt for Wendy Harmer's breakfast radio show! I was known as the man on the street, and on this morning I could have been landing on it....

Wendy arrived at 2Day FM in early 1993 and soon she'd be dominating the breakfast ratings with co-hosts Peter Moon, Jamie Dunn and my mate Paul Holmes for 84 of the following 88 ratings surveys.

She told News Corp: "The best thing about rating well for so long is that you get to have a little room where you can lock the door and keep management out."

"If you're not rating well, they're in your ear all day long saying, 'Why don't you do this?'"

But one was simply beyond the pale, as she explained to news.com.au, the line had to be drawn on these 'doozies.'

"There's an old radio stunt where you get a paddock, you

The best thing about working for the Wendy Harmer (top left) breakfast show and the whole gang at 2Day was reuniting with my good friends Ron E Sparx, Paul Holmes and Mike Hammond, seen here in a special Mothers' Day broadcast.

divide it up into squares, you put a cow in it and wherever it drops a cow pat, the person with that number wins a million dollars," said Harmer.

"When I was about to have my baby, a couple of people at 2Day FM thought that if I could just do that with my baby, it would be a great stunt."

There was another stunt she recalled that required the heavy involvement of yours truly, as she told of one escape that went horribly wrong.

"I remember our man on the street, Frank Vincent, he was in this stunt called *Dash for Cash.*

We pinned money all over him and sent him out to a park and the idea was that you had to catch him to win the cash.

"But there were a lot of highly trained athletes who rocked up and they caught him within 20 metres and they almost killed him."

I've always wanted to be 'rolling in it' but this wasn't quite what I had in mind. Wendy wasn't kidding when she referred to my near death. To this day a walk through Parramatta Plaza brings back chilling memories of how I almost shuffled off the mortal coil under the great weight of bodies. I can recall as if it were yesterday how piece by piece the sky above me was being blacked-out before security guards joined horrified on-lookers in rescuing me from a

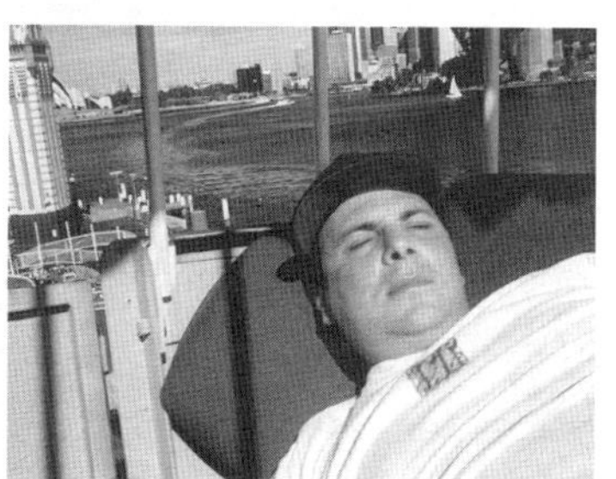

Of all my crazy assignments as the Man on the Street at 2DayFM this was proudest achievement, sitting on a Ferris Wheel for 2100 rotations in a vigil to help save Sydney's historic Luna Park. I may have been forgiven for thinking my career was going in circles, but it was serious fun as a range of Sydney celebrities joined me on the ride.

permanent departure more akin to the ill fate of those caught in the most manic of mosh pits. Wendy called me for a welfare check after the show, and her relief about my survival, which was seeming unlikely at one stage, was palpable.

Wendy was a great operator, and extremely funny. While she didn't share Doug's caustic tongue, hers was sharp all the same, with perfect comic timing, and a real team player when it came to weaving seamlessly with the whole crew. I loved being part of the team and had a great relationship with Wendy. She was somewhat a rarity in commercial radio, a self-described 'old lefty' who championed women's rights, opposed the republic, and advocated for the underdog as a panellist advising the Australian government on the National Disability Strategy. She was a true renaissance woman, and it was a complete delight to work with such a passionate powerhouse of creativity, comedy and compassion.

I was interested to read recently that she tunes into 2DayFM occasionally these days and laments what she considered to be the over-reliance on celebrity interviews, regarding them as the icing on the cake.

"I mean, who cares about some Hollywood celeb when you can turn Carol and Brian from Beaconsfield into the real stars?"

She recalled the hysterical talkback segment: 'How did you catch out your lover having an affair?

"This woman rang up and said, 'My husband told me that he was going out for a night on the town with his mate Brian, and I knew that wasn't true, because I was in bed with Brian at the time."

I was having a wonderful time at 2Day FM as the *Man on the Street* and was even seconded to cover the surfing beat as *The Reporter in the Water*. When I think of the highlights – they literally didn't come much higher than the Ferris Wheel at Sydney's Luna Park.

That's where I was perched with my microphone for four days to support the public campaign to prevent the closure of the historic amusement destination on Lavender Bay in the shadows of the Harbour Bridge's northern pylons.

The restoration of Luna Park had started two years earlier, starting with the famous smiling face being moved back to the entrance.

For the next six months a small army of tradesmen and artists worked feverishly on restoring and repairing the park's buildings and signature murals.

Local apartment residents were furious about noise of a 40 metre steel roller coaster and an open air car park and the park was besieged by legal claims from protesters and those who tenders with unsuccessful bids for the redevelopment.

Then the newly elected Labor State Government delivered a hammer blow by scrapping its guarantee of a $14 million loan to the Luna Park Trust, before appointing an administrator to replace its board of directors. The park was forced to close again on 14 February 1996 but not before I played my own unique role in trying to save an institution that had entertained Sydney families since 1935.

The appreciation of my *Man on the Street* broadcasts from the Ferris Wheel was expressed in the below letter from Luna Park management in May 1995.

Dear Frank,

Just a note to thank you for your support during our recent campaign to keep Luna Park open and for riding the Ferris Wheel – what a guy!

As you well know the government has granted the Park a reprieve and has appointed an administrator, James Millar of Ernst & Young to oversee the government's interests.

We believe that the public support that flowed for the Park – 50,000 petitioners, the efforts of the Luna Park staff, Friends of the Park and the community in general all helped to encourage the Government to reconsider its position.

Once again thank you for your support as it made a difference. As I have said you have earned the right to be a 'lunatic' for life.

Anytime you want to visit the Park please ring me so I can organise your tickets.

Thanks again Frank.

Jacqui Wade
Public Affairs Manager
Luna Park Amusements

LUNA PARK
JUST FOR FUN!

16 May 1995

Frank Vincent
Radio 2DAYFM
220 Pacific Highway
Crows Nest NSW 2065

Dear Frank,

Just a note to thank you for your support during our recent campaign to keep Luna Park open and for riding the Ferris Wheel - what a guy!

As you well know the government has granted the Park a reprieve and has appointed an administrator, James Millar of Ernst & Young to oversee the governments interests.

We believe that the public support that flowed for the Park - 50,000 petitioners, the efforts of the Luna Park staff, Friends of the Park and the community in general all helped to encourage the Government to reconsider its position.

Once again thank you for your support as it made a difference. As I have said you have earned the right to be a 'lunatic' for life. Anytime you want to visit the Park please ring me so I can organise your tickets. Thanks again Frank.

Kind regards,

Jacqui Wade
Public Affairs Manager
Luna Park Amusements

The management of Luna Park expresses its appreciation.

The park would go back into mothballs until reopening again in 2004, but by that stage I had been saddened to read the original Harmer crew had gone their separate ways after a somewhat bitter falling out.

Peter Moon headed back to Melbourne after what was described as 'creative differences' with Wendy, and Jamie Dunn – the voice of the cheeky television Puppet Agro – headed north for a new dawn in his career on Brisbane radio, where he was more popular than ever. It was great to see Jamie succeed in his own right. For so long his fame had been sheeted home to the furry creation with a mono brow on his right hand as a fixture on breakfast TV, and finally it was time for the alter ego to move aside. The seamlessness of the banter on air belied the real tension between Wendy and Jamie when the mics were switched-off. It was a credit to their professionalism in vowing to get the job done regardless of the

With Foreigner lead singer Lou Gramm and colleague, the late Lou Dimovitch.

loathing them seemed to have for one another.

Then in 2003 Wendy called it a day at 2Day.

As Merrick Watts said after he and Nova partner Rosso had taken Wendy's breakfast crown:

"It's very hard to imagine doing breakfast radio that long and being that good at it."

"It's incredible she's done so well for so long."

There was no shock to see Wendy playing a big part in delivering ABC Radio record audience numbers for the breakfast slot after she team-up with Robbie Buck in 2015. She was the ultimate professional. Few announcers can boast her success in commercial *and public* radio. It was an honour to be part of her team at 2Day. But just one thing Wendy – please make sure they put all that cash in my pockets next time. *Nobody will catch me!*

CHAPTER 11

REDLINE REV-HEAD RAT

I felt immense gratitude towards 2DayFM for effectively rescuing my career after the undignified Triple M exit but there could be no doubt I was forced to make serious compromises on my burning ambition to continue sport reporting.

Unlike Triple M 2DayFM didn't consider sport to be of any interest to its listeners, and it was strictly off limits for me as I maintained my duties as *The Man on the Street*. It was a gig that buoyed my profile, but I'd be lying to say it left me with a great deal of professional satisfaction. It's not the sort of segment I would not tune into myself, so it had the feel of an acting role. But like any 'burger flipper' – I believed that just because *you cooked the shit* didn't mean you *had to eat it!*

I would maintain my involvement in sport as a spectator only and Rugby League ground announcer for the Canterbury Bankstown Bulldogs and Cronulla Sharks, and my great passion was no longer what had previously amounted to a paid hobby. That meant travelling to the United States on my own coin in 1994 for the FIFA world Cup. I was keen to see how this ultimate sporting tournament operated and was thrilled to attend games in Los Angeles and San Francisco, meeting up with my old SBS mate Andy Paschalidis.

I found San Francisco to be somewhat underwhelming. Over the decades it had been built up in my mind as a fantastic, vibrant city, but I was surprised by its relatively small size, the extent of overt poverty, the number of homeless people and the shabby shape of a weather beaten Golden Gate Bridge. In short, I thought it was overrated, and a far cry from the nirvana all the postcards and publicity would have had me believe. No wonder those 'little cable cars only went *halfway* to the stars'! Tony Bennett was right, but wrong in so many other ways. I was never going to leave my heart there. Maybe I was spoiled – being from Sydney – but our own harbour city leaves the Californian version in the shade of a grey day created by Frisco's famous fog. As Mark Twain once said: "*The coldest winter I ever spent was a summer in San Francisco*". It left me cold alright.

TV career launch, reporting for Channel Ten's RPM.

In contrast – the World Cup was heating-up. It was an exhilarating contest, hosted at nine venues across the US. It would end in triumph for Brazil in 3–2 victory against Italy, decided by a penalty shootout at Pasadena's Rose Bowl near LA. It was fantastic to be part of what turned out to be an historic event, the most profitable and attracting the largest crowd in World Cup history. There was an astounding of 68,991 spectators per game – a record that stood until 2018.

But soccer wasn't the only sport on my mind during this American adventure. Unimpressed with San Francisco I decided to evacuate and head to Houston to try my luck for a seat at the deciding NBA basketball final between the New York Knicks and the Houston Rockets at the latter's home stadium in Texas. The small matter of not having a ticket didn't deter me in the least. Such was my manic determination not to miss this great event.

I had become passionate about basketball since the days of forging a close association with the Sydney Kings while covering the sport for Triple M. The opportunity to see the game played by its very best players was too delicious to resist. Trouble was – the opportunity was limited on account of having no clue about how I would force myself into the Summit Stadium.

In a celebrity 50cc bike race at Sydney's Eastern Creek for the Australian 500cc Motorcycle Grand Prix.

The Summit was at the base of an adjoining hotel, so step one was to book a room. Step 2? Well, there was *no* step 2. Not that I was aware of anyway.

On game day, June 22, 1994, I hung around the foyer to scope out the entrances – and then grabbed my chance.

Three burly security guards formed a wall of muscle as they walked into the arena, and I just followed them in. It was bold but beautiful for its simplicity. Nobody asked any questions. The view of my arrival had been totally obscured by the man mountains who led the way. Luckily not one of them turned around to see me in their formidable slipstream. I was standing by all the while to trot out my broadest Aussie accent and simply play dumb under any sudden interrogation. But security cameras notwithstanding I remained undetected while making my way stealthily to the giant press box, looking like I belonged there, helping myself to the drinks and food laid on for the media, and slipping inconspicuously into the scene as if I were on the job back home.

There was one last challenge though – to secure a spare seat overlooking the actual court. This was the seventh and deciding game of the finals, and the showdown was bound to attract the biggest press contingent of the series hitherto. There was one reserved seat next to the chair allocated for the New York Post reporter. It had been reserved for whoever was coming for *The Sacramento Bee* daily newspaper. I figured this would be my best shot for a seat, and waited until about five minutes before the opening whistle to ask the guy from the *Post*: "Mate what time does the *Sacramento Bee* journo usually show-up?" The *Post* reporter delivered the news for which I had been silently praying.

"Man, The Bee reporter has not turned up to a *single game* – and I don't expect to see them here today."

I couldn't believe my luck. I had one of the best seats in the house, and I was being watered and fed! I'm only hoping this belated revelation doesn't inspire the NBA to send me a back-dated invoice – with interest!

The game itself was as scintillating as I anticipated. Memories of the encounter are vivid to this day, as you might well imagine when you're witnessing the world's best basketballers move their huge frames around a small wooden floor with blinding, brutal speed and unerring precision. No wonder some compared this spectacle to a 'dance.' This was *basketball ballet* at its best – and while none of these performers needed to stand on their toes for added height – they had to be on them for every second of a game always ready to punish the slightest lapse in concentration.

In a genuine nailbiter the Rockets beat the Knicks 90–84, denying the New York side the double of securing the NBA and NHL championships in the same year. It was Houston's first NBA championship title, and the town went mad.

The Houston Post

CHAMP CITY!

Rockets gift-wrap title for Houston

The day after I snuck into to see The Rockets ride to the top of the NBA, I had the front page of the local paper autographed by the great Houston point guard Kenny Smith.

It had been a nerve-wracking night – mixed with the excitement of witnessing history while knowing I had no right to be there. Talk about hiding in plain sight. At one stage the reporter for the David Letterman show, famous saxophonist Branford Marsalis, approached me after hearing my accent. He then took me into the NBC box and introduced me. I definitely needed an introduction, because unlike every other media person at the Summit I didn't have a name tag!

I souvenired the next day's *Houston Post*, featuring Rockets star Kenny Smith on the cover. Years later Kenny was in Sydney for a promotional game and was kind enough to sign the same front page I had kept in mint condition. It remains among my more prized possessions.

To be a very small part of the NBA and World Cup finals was way more than enough to reignite the determination to resume my own career in sport. That opportunity would arrive in the form of my very first job in television.

I had been harassing the head of Fox sports Saul Shtein for a gig. He was a veteran of television sport, making his name as an executive producer of test and one day cricket, Rugby League, Formula 1, Wimbledon, thoroughbred racing coverage, boxing, surfing and Channel 9's Wide World of Sports.

He went on to lead Channel 7 sport, and headed-up coverage of three Summer and two Winter Olympic games, and production of AFL, and the Australian Open tennis.

It was indeed an honour to be hired by such an industry legend, and I was excited to be learning TV production from the ground up on the national cable broadcaster. I began as a producer, working closely with the head of Fox sports News Bob de la Lande, the former 7 Network United States correspondent and senior reporter on National Nine News.

Things got off to amusing start, and nobody laughed harder than Saul when I stood up at the end of a production meeting only to knock the light switch with my shoulder and leave the room in darkness. The boss was mightily amused, and his warm response would turn out to be misleading, to say the least.

Before long I was up to speed on the finer points of writing and voicing the pictures, and editing, while covering the range of major sports news – including motor sport – still one of my favourites long after my enthusiastic and frequent filing of stories on Triple M, where my passion for car racing was inflamed by that High Priest of the Rev Heads Doug Mulray.

It was my love of cars that actually led to my sudden departure from Fox Sports News.

I had recently taken possession of red convertible BMW 325. It was my pride and joy, a magnificent driving machine that I treated like a favourite child. Upon learning my baby was to lose her parking space within the safe shelter of the Fox Sports News carpark in Pyrmont I just lost it, foolishly venting my anger to none other than Saul Shtein. He explained that spaces had to be made available for the stars of Super League making guest appearances in panel shows. But my foolhardy opposition to the idea was at the time non-negotiable. I thought there was simply no way my glistening mean machine could be exposed to the public in street parking. It was way too pretty, and an absolute magnet for resentful vandals. The idea that it should be exposed to such dangers was unthinkable, and unthinkingly, I gave one of the most powerful TV sports executives in the country what might as well have been a hot blast from the Beemer's twin exhausts. He waited until I was finished – and fired me. The cold blooded henchmen from the Orwellian Human Resources department didn't use the parking row as the official reason for my sacking, finding some other excuse to send me on my way with a lousy cheque for $4,000.

Just 900 metres to the west of the Fox Studios was Channel TEN. It didn't have any staff parking either, but it did have a lifeline. It had become the official rights holder for the coverage of motor sports and suddenly this hot headed hog was finding heaven.

TEN offered me a reporting gig on its program RPM, hosted by veteran radio and TV journo Bill Woods and the legendary late Barry Sheene, a two time World 500cc Motorcycle Grand Prix champion. As far as a men's sheds go this 'garage' was as good it gets for a natural born rev head, even if there was no room for my beloved Beemer in the actual underground carpark.

Bill Woods is a delightful bloke. 'Accomplished', 'professional' and 'gentleman' are the three words I immediately associate with Bill, a rare breed of broadcaster – displaying great ability as a writer and presenter without a whiff of smug, aloof self-satisfaction.

Bill's readiness to help me steer my career into what seemed its natural home made my transition to the TV medium complete. Bill was a masterful 'script doctor', tweaking here and there until the story was close to perfection for voicing-over. He taught me so much about how the economical use of words could make for an effective and entertaining turn of phrase. Woodsy as he was affectionately known, had honed his craft for neat, tight and punchy writing as a veteran of radio, starting in Sydney as a reporter and newsreader at 2WS after arriving via country radio on a path well-worn by the both of us. Our rapport was instant, and I'll always be in his debt for the guidance and time he afforded me as I settled into the TEN motorsports team.

The tuition was having an immediate and stunning impact. My career was about to be 'redlining' – the term used for a car engine revving above its rated maximum revolutions per minute to shoot into the red zone of a tachometer.

TEN had the rights to cover the World Rally Championships, and in no time I was flying business class to Europe to produce a documentary about Australian driver Michael Guest. On the strength of winning a stage on the Australian leg of the World Championships Guest was invited to compete with the best in Europe. Even he would admit he was probably not Australia's best rally driver at the time, but his good looks and personality made for ideal TV talent, and I was assigned to deliver two one hour episodes of an RPM doco devoted to his great adventure on the global stage. That meant travelling to Spain, Portugal, the UK, New Zealand, China, Cyrus and Finland to shoot what was titled *The Guest Quest*. It was amazing to be sampling so many rich cultures, but a conspicuous when the culinary sensation of tasting open flamed chicken with spicey sauces, washed down with a glass of Tinto red wine in the city of Porto. I can still taste it, a memory that's refreshed every time I have a glass of similar pinot noir. Then there was the unforgettable day of shooting the spectacular Great Wall in China as a podium presentation was staged with this wonder of the world as a backdrop. What a set!

Rally driving was a revelation. My first close-up look at this competition convinced me this was motor racing at its best, combining the grunt and growl of tough, nimble machines with the guts, guile and stamina of whip smart drivers.

The best way to get a true appreciation of the skills required for success in this gruelling, dangerous sport was to sit in the navigator's seat next to world champion Richard Burns, the only Englishman to win it as a driver in 2001. Trying to stay calm and appear cool as pine trees whizzed past the passenger side window in a frightening blur made a rattlesnake roller-coaster seem like a Ferriss wheel. I was a picture of stark terror, but to scream or even so much as dig my fingernails into the dashboard of his flying Ralliart Mitsubishi would be an insult to the master at the wheel. I was in fact in the best of hands.

Tragically four years after winning the World Championship the quietly spoken Burns died of a brain tumour. He was only 34. I cried when the news of his passing arrived on November 25, 2005. Among the many tributes was high praise from Jeremy Clarkson, the former host of *Top Gear*, where Burns would appear as a program favourite to claim rallying was more exciting and influential than Formula One. He was right. Rally drivers are the Special Forces of motor racing. Formula One drivers just have to drive.

Until now my familiarity with the top drawer of motor sport had been confined to the Bathurst production car endurance race and the fledgling V-8 supercars. Rallying was an exciting new world that would change my life in ways I had never imagined.

The proud nation of Finland would always been on my bucket list of destinations, and that's exactly where I found myself – in a heavily forest land famous for a pedigree of drivers known as *The Flying Finns*. They ruled the dusty, muddy tracks of world rallying for an incredible four decades.

The fans mark their drivers hard in Finland. You're not even rated a champion until you've won *four* world titles. It's as natural a habitat for rally drivers as Switzerland is for skiers, with 75 percent of the Finnish landscape covered with forest. Add an almost unfathomable 187,888 lakes and it's little wonder navigating this land in a car requires a great deal of skill even as an amateur motorist!

I loved Finland, especially the upper northern reaches of this proud country – and that's an admiration I share with millions of kids! This remote region happens to be the home of Santa Clause – AKA Lapland. Lapland is a magical corner of the world, populated by the native Sami tribes, a small but hardy race of people, known for their unique headwear, reindeer herding and wicked sense of humour. I was told by every Sami I met that: "*We have a saying here. In summer we fish and fuck. In winter we don't fish.*" While in Lapland I found myself in the lap of wonderful hospitality, courtesy of the Pohjahovi Hotel in the city Rovaniemi. They were magnificent digs with a spectacular view of the picturesque.

With Tommy Makinen, Finland's four-time World Rally champion.

Kemijoki river, and I'll never forget the hotel's fabulous old style timber sauna and jacuzzi where I joined five other successful adults, sitting around in our birthday suits in what was known as the Icebreakers Club, getting to know each other before I decided it was too hot – and I hurled myself into a nearby lake for the hyperthermic shock of my life. When I jumped through a thin layer of ice It sounded as though I had put my feet through a pane of glass – and it was just as sharp as the blood flowed into the freezing waters, to raise the serious concern among my new friends. When I noticed the blood I found two cuts to my ankles. It turned out they were minor lacerations – and I lost more pride than blood as I hobbled back to firmer ground.

I ended up in Lapland after travelling with the Mitsubishi rally team to test their vehicle ahead of the approaching winter events, such as the Arctic Rally and The Rally of Sweden. Lapland provided perfect conditions for the trials, with its daily temperature plunging to minus 22 degrees Celsius. It was just as well – because upon landing in Sweden the drivers had contend with snow up to a metre deep, requiring tyres with spikes, sturdy oil sumps and rubber hoses that wouldn't perish. This was more like ice skating than driving, and bad news for cameras – prone to all sorts of malfunctions in the deep freeze. Fortunately, the Finns knew how to keep themselves well insulated with their favourite alcoholic beverage Koskenkorva vodka, always handy in copious amounts to take the edge off the frostbite. I was so fond of this drink that my Finnish friends were already to replenish my supplies when they visited Australia. Those mates included Pekka Kaidesoja, a production director at Finland's public broadcaster YLE.

I was fortunate to see one of the modern day Flying Finns Tommi Mäkinen going blow for blow with Richard Burns in Finland while making the doco about Guest, who did his best against stiff competition by finishing in the top 20 on several occasions, ahead of 110 other competitors.

One of my saddest assignments was being sent to the Goodwood Motor Festival of Speed where many big name drivers and frustrated rev heads meet annually to test their skills on a professional circuit. The Goodwood Festival patrons included Nick Mason of Pink Floyd drumming fame, swapping the beating of pig skin for the burning of rubber. I was amazed to see just how many amateur enthusiasts turned up to mix it with the big boys.

I was there to announce a tribute to Barry Sheene after he was diagnosed with cancer, and had the honour of interviewing many motor sport greats in a wave of unanimous, glowing praise for the 500cc legend.

I was very familiar with Barry's traditional stomping grounds, attending dozens of 500cc motor sport events and meeting all the major formula champions, including Wayne Raney and Eddie Lawson. I've got great memories from the launch of Wayne Raney's biography, a signed copy he handed to me personally as many great past and present riders gathered at Donnington raceway to celebrate his decorated career.

Then there was the evening of celebrating the 300th victory of Michelin Tyres and I had the delight of meeting Jack Finlay, the

Aussie who helped develop the company's famous slicks.

With Australia's five time World 500cc Motorcycle Champion Mick Doohan.

One of my more amusing encounters with champion rally drivers involved very witty French master Didier Auriol. He won the world championship in 1994 in his trademark Celica Turbo 4WD and I met him at the height of his powers. A superb competitor, he also proved to be a great sport when it came to my cheeky questions, delivering one of the best comeback lines I've ever heard.

He was dressed in a white driving suit, and I remarked:

"Didier, have you ever been told you look great in white!" to which he replied: "I look good in *any* colour!"

I guess bravado and quick thinking go with the rugged territory that such a driver has to navigate at frightening speed to succeed at his level. I should have expected no less!

Another one of my favourite Moto GP stars was Italian Valentino Rossi. He was always approachable, and never refused an interview. I recall once at Phillip Island he was at a local pub playing pool with his teammates, and I challenged him before kicking his ass! He took the hiding sportingly, but he was more concerned with winning the Australian Moto GP 250cc class and he did indeed go on to take the chequered flag, a far more appealing square of material than a length of green felt.

It was a great weekend. There was a sea of motorcycles in the

Reuniting with Santa Claus in Lapland, with the Finnish Mitsubishi test team.

carpark as tens of thousands of Australians arrived on their two and four wheelers to see Michael Doohan bag his fifth world 500cc championship.

Doohan's highly anticipated duel with Max Biaggi didn't eventuate after the Italian finished 8th. Biaggi had been cast as the black hatted rider in this race, and Doohan's fans didn't hide their dislike of him. The rivalry was captured by a message painted on the back window of a spectator's utility, which read: "Go Mick – Biaggi is a wanker." Welcome to Australia Max! I can assure you you're not the first Italian to be on the wrong side of coarse Aussie profanity. This Fairfield wog knows all about it!

The so-called low budget Network Channel TEN wasn't sparing any expense with the coverage of motorsports. The sponsorships that came with it enabled me to fly business class for every trip to Europe, and while my monthly salary was a relative pittance compared to what I had been earning, and as improbable as it seemed at the time

I was living a high enough life, mixing it with the jet setting drivers and their teams. I was heading to far flung, scenic corners of Spain, Portugal, Finland, the UK and New Zealand – covering a sport I loved and somebody else was picking up the bill. Then there was the time the whole RPM team headed for Greece. My passport had more stamps than a rockstar's! Before then I'd only join the ideas of motor racing and travel in my head by thinking of the drive along the Great Western Highway from Sydney to Bathurst for the annual touring car classic.

The experience I was getting in TV production was invaluable, but although I was comfortable with voicing-over the stories in using my decades of radio experience I was still very nervous in front the camera. I don't mean as one of two heads in an interview situation but looking right down the barrel. The lens might as well have been a gun. For some reason my customary confidence abandoned me whenever the camera was rolling, and I would avoid it whenever I could. My unease on camera just about defines the ultimate occupational hazard for a television reporter!

After two years of freelancing as TEN's globe-trotting motoring correspondent I landed a job at the 7 Network and was now playing with the big boys of Australian television, filing daily on a variety of sports in the evening bulletins. I worked with some legends of Australian sports journalism, including the world's leading Rugby commentator at the time Gordon Bray. He was the consummate Mr Nice Guy, always obliging in showing me the ropes of reporting for a major network. But I remained out of my comfort zone and started scanning the horizon for other opportunities.

My travels throughout Europe and the United States had left me with hankering for taking-on challenges in the wider world. Don't be mistaken – I love Australia, and at the time I had bought a beautiful home in the inner Sydney suburb of Leichhardt. But I was aching for more adventure – and motor racing, basketball and soccer were all competing for the front of my mind's grid. I was passionate about all three – and determined to be back in the thick of covering these sports on the world stage.

CHAPTER 12

LAND OF THE GIANTS

For someone who is not terribly tall I can hardly be accused of having a complex about my height...if only the company I've been keeping for many years is any indication.

When the Australian National Basketball League was established in 1979 basketball – like baseball – was one example of how insidious American imperialism in the form of popular culture had *not* exactly succeeded down under. Australians were happy to watch American television, but had always balked at embracing American football, baseball and to a lesser degree basketball.

Before the NBL was up and running there were two national basketball competitions – the national titles and championships – but the nation's interest in the sport only stirred in a significant way when Australia would compete in the summer Olympic Games. Apart from that occasional attention every four years Aussies mainly identified with the sport through shooting hoops at high school when kids were becoming tall enough to be half a chance of landing a basket. It simply had not been woven tightly into our daily culture in the same way the limited land availability in big American cities guaranteed strong recreational participation by kids of all ages looking to expend energy in the ''hood' where tightly packed apartment buildings demanded an escape to the outdoors, even if they weren't so great.

I guess Australia has never suffered from a lack of space, and our kids were more likely to be playing cricket in backyards their counterparts in crowded American cities could only dream about.

That would explain why so many champion American baseballers came from the regional areas. Baseball fields in Manhattan for example could only be found in places like Central Park, and there simply weren't enough to go around. Basketball on the other hand could be squeezed onto a street corner, in between crowded tenements – and half courts or just a brick wall with a hoop could help kids hone their skills and accuracy.

With the GOAT Michael Jordan and Ahmad Rashad, the Bulls Court announcer and long standing great of the living legend, who took the time for me to grab a few words and pose for this photo at Le Mans in France. This happy snap is one of my prized possessions.

So transplanting basketball into mainstream Australian sport was always going to be a major challenge – and the sport's administrators believed a structured national competition based on the US NBA would inspire a brand new wave of interest. Until then our familiarity with American basketball had been largely confined within the fuss created by the Harlem Globetrotters when they would arrive on their world tour as a quasi-circus act.

Nine years after the Australian NBL was launched we witnessed the arrival of the Sydney Kings, formed in a merger between the Western Sydney Westars and the Sydney Supersonics. As a serious if not overly ambitious signal of intent looked to the Los Angeles Lakers for their purple and gold colours.

Reporting sport for Triple M at the time I was one of the few journalists to afford the Kings constant coverage as they battled for media attention, at one stage even paying one daily newspaper for editorial space.

I got to know the team well, including Damien Keough and star American recruit Steve Carfino, who became a trail blazer for promoting the game in Australia, starting with the Hobart Devils and named as a member of the All NBL first team in his debut season after his scoring averaged 34.7 per game. After two seasons in Tasmania Carfino was poached by the Kings American coach Bob Turner and the former Boston Celtic continued to dominate the NBL ranks for steals and assists. Ongoing back problems forced his early retirement in 1991 and Steve went on to become a leading TV commentator.

Melbourne born Sydney captain Damien Keough was a home grown star, having already built a strong national profile as a veteran of the 1984 and 1988 Olympic Games. He would end up playing 207 games for Australia, also competing in three world championships in a stellar 13 year international career that began in 1981. Tim Morrissey also became a great mate. He was very popular with the fans – but not in Melbourne, where he was punched by a spectator in a corporate box in 1995, and that was the year after he was elbowed by one of the Melbourne Tigers in an outrageous court foul. Understandably Tim never liked venturing south of the border. He went on to become a Sports Editor for *The Daily Telegraph.*

For the Kings to promote Keough and Carfino was a marketing masterstroke, a combination of Steve's dash of Hollywood and Damien's homegrown hero celebrity started pulling big crowds. Add the 'Ritchie Cunningham' looks of coach Bob Turner and you could well say it was a case of 'Happy Days' for the Sydney Kings as the

From my personal collection of photos from the home of the Bulls, Chicago's United Center during the 1996 finals, where super model Cindy Crawford was marvelling at her autographed Michael Jordan Singlet. Below — the Great Man again and the colourful and controversial Dennis Rodman.

fledgling franchise began to make its mark. In fact, I was the one who christened Bob 'Ritchie Cunningham', and it stuck, with the avuncular American always ready to have a laugh about the attention I drew to his doppelgänger.

I was proud to be heavily involved in supporting the Kings, travelling with the team on road trips and reporting all their games with prominence on Sydney's top rating commercial radio station.

Like Triple M the Kings were new and fresh. It was a great match.

The city's imagination was starting to be captured when the Kings became the first Sydney team to make the NBL play-offs by finishing in the final four of the 1989 season. They defeated the Melbourne Tigers 2–1 in the playoffs before a 60 point thrashing at the hands of the Canberra Cannons in the third and series deciding game.

I remember once inviting them all to a barbecue at my place in Leichhardt and wondering whether my small backyard Weber could handle the great slabs of prime steak they brought along. To my great relief the baby Weber did the job as the boys agreed the meat was cooked to perfection. After the barbie the players signed a Kings calendar saying: To Frank – the Weber BBQ King – good luck!" I guess being a BBQ King was close as I'd get to becoming a *Sydney* King. They were forever grateful for my patronage, and readiness to join them in sharing the glory of the cheers and the pain of the tears as we cried into our beers at Liverpool's Collingwood Hotel on the long, miserable trip from Canberra after the Canons thumping. There was another episode at Melbourne airport when we were downing Bloody Marys for breakfast in a bid to sober-up, but we weren't quite straightened as the temptation of the coin operated toy elephant, horse and truck rides – designed for children – proved too much for these big kids. Maybe Beroccas would have been a better idea than the tomato juice and vodka hangover 'solution'! We made for quite a sight and luckily airport security was not doing RBT on the rides – because we would have immediately lost our licence for cheap thrills....

Looking back, it was just as well the antics on the kids' rides at Tullamarine preceded the days of social media. If such an escapade had occurred these days it would have gone viral – and sponsors would have been arcing up deluxe, and never mind the real prospect that yours truly would be facing unemployment!

In Barcelona with giant Australian Boomers Luc Longley, John Dorge and Leroy Loggins.

I couldn't wait to get back to the United States to see more NBA, and when the Houston Rockets lined-up against the Orlando Magic to successfully mount their bid for back-to-back titles in 1995 I returned to the Summit, but this time I had all the necessary passes. I didn't have to sweat on a no-show from *The Sacramento Bee*. It was another unforgettable experience, coinciding with the cinematic Houston premiere of the movie Apollo 13. And who should be sitting in the front row just metres away from me? Ron Howard – doing his Bob Turner impersonation – and the stars of the film Tom Hanks, Val Kilmer and Kevin Bacon. But all three would be dwarfed – literally and figuratively by the biggest man I had ever seen. The gigantic Shaquille O'Neal. The guy was even more massive than I had imagined, but his bulk wouldn't be enough to rescue the Magic as they went down by 12 points to the home team.

Don't get me wrong, I love my rugby league and cricket as much as any red-blooded Aussie male, but I have forever been bemused by how the sport of the world's most famous athlete could be considered a minority affair in Australia.

The world's leading manufacturer of sportswear wasn't short in its appreciation of having their merchandise promoted by a basket balling god but for some reason this great sport was flat out making a headline in the Australian press, in the face of growing participation rates and the enormous popularity of Michael Jordan across the planet.

There can be no doubt MJ set a great example for Australian children, yet our national media maintained a blind eye to what was so glaringly obvious to the rest of the world.

To this day, I find it difficult to believe that I was just among a handful of journalists to give basketball the recognition it commanded, so effortlessly everywhere else.

My early association with the Sydney Kings, stimulated my lifelong passion for basketball. My admiration would lead me to leave Australia and cover the NBA for three years as our own players began to make a huge name for themselves on the American stage.

There was none bigger than Chicago Bulls recruit Luc Longley The West Australian giant was playing alongside Jordan, Dennis Rodman and Scottie Pippen as the Chicago Bulls won three NBA titles on the spin in a dominant era celebrated recently in the blockbusting Netflix series *The Last Dance*. Longley's rise to superstardom led me to connect with Perth's 96FM to provide West Australians with regular updates on news about their hometown hero.

After a brief stint with the Perth Wildcats the first chapter of Luc's American fairy tale was written with a contract at college level with the New Mexico Lobos. In 1991 he was drafted 7th by the Minnesota Timberwolves and traded to the Bulls three years later before lining-up as Chicago's starting centre in the 1995–96 season in which the team made history with an NBA record for the most wins in a regular season. Longley was seen as integral to that success and remained in the starting line-up throughout the legendary championship three-peat.

I had a one-on-one interview with Luc at the time. After I asked him about exactly how he got the Bulls he explained that after training with the Timberwolves one day the coach called him to say: "Luc I've got some good news and bad news. You've been traded to the Bulls."

He would wrap up his US career in much shorter engagements with the Phoenix Suns and New York Knicks. Sadly at the height of his fame in Chicago an ankle injury prevented him from joining the Australian Boomers in the 1996 Atlanta Olympics.

At game one of the 96 series in Seattle I asked Michael Jordan at the press conference how he thought Luc might perform. The legend replied: "He's had a great season and he'll be fine." I thought just to get an answer from the great man at such a crowded press conference was an achievement in itself. There were so many journalists there I prepared thoroughly by asking an NBA media official which side the Bulls would be sitting at the players' table. I made sure I was sitting opposite and was in poll position to launch my solitary question for the Australian audience. At the press conference I was introduced to some of America's leading sports writers, including Rick Telander – famous for his back page column in Sports Illustrated America. Rick was a little aloof to begin with, but he melted once I told him I had spent the day at Renton Cemetery paying my respects to the great guitarist Jimi Hendrix. Rick inquired about directions to the gravesite, and it turned out we were both Hendrix devotees – and he was planning his own pilgrimage to the resting place of the rock 'n' roll legend. During my visit to the cemetery, I found three Swedish musicians at the Hendrix memorial, rolling a joint and obligingly they offered me what I thought was a harmless puff. This was powerful weed in state where recreational use has long been legal. As if interviewing the greatest basketballer of all time a few hours later wasn't enough of a head spin! No wonder I was so relaxed at the press conference. In the front of the entire Bulls team, I didn't skip a beat. I like Seattle, the home of great bands such as Nirvana and Sound Garden, and while I was there the sports journo surrendered to the old rock jock and I was compelled to swing by The Crocodile Club to watch Electrafixion – once known as Echo & the Bunnymen, famous for their moody movie music – and at the vanguard of 1990s grunge.

I shuttled back-and-forth across the Pacific regularly to report mainly on the all-conquering Bulls. There would be no need to repeat my gate-crashing efforts in Houston. I was a fully accredited member of the American basketball press, with a pass that afford me access to all areas, including the Bulls dressing rooms in the United Centre – the setting for so much of their spectacular success.

The scenes at the United Center were surreal to say the least. I looked up at one stage to see supermodel Cindy Crawford walking straight past me after she'd been presented with a Michael Jordan jersey by Dennis Rodman. Then out of nowhere Charlie Sheen approached me and I asked him to say a big hello to his fans in Australia. He obliged enthusiastically, grabbing my mobile phone and saying: "Hello Australia – this is Charlie Sheen!" The following weekend he saw me at a Cubs baseball game, and incredibly he recognised me – saying you're that Aussie! It made my day.

What do you think Michael Jordan and Audrey Hepburn might have in common – apart from sharing the mantle of 20th century iconic star status? Well – as Audrey once famously said: "Paris is always a good idea." And MJ just happened to agree whenever he needed to escape the unrelenting scrutiny of a nation while living in home country.

He would later disclose to thesportsrush.com: "I used to go to Paris a lot 'cause Paris was a place I could just walk on the streets. I could sit down and have dinner or have lunch or whatever and people never really paid attention. I loved to do that. I just stayed outside out there. I wouldn't want to go inside at all. I just loved sitting out and watching people."

Clearly wealth and fame were not always easy for the big man.

As for what I had in common with Michael? Well, that came as a total shock. Turned out we both absolutely adored motor sport. MJ was particularly fond of 500cc Grand Prix Motorcycle Racing at a time when I was covering the heroics of four time Australian champion Mick Doohan.

I arrived at Charles de Gaulle Airport in June 1996 for Channel 10's *RPM* I noticed Suzuki team leader Garry Stewart at the baggage carousel. I had met Garry before but wasn't sure he'd remember me.

In the spirit of my lifelong theme to always 'have a go' I called-out his name.

He turned around to say: "Frank! How are you? Great to see you." So good in fact that he offered to take me to Le Mans in his own vehicle, provided I would drive. Along the way he announced the Suzuki team was going to be hosting a very special guest at its trackside workshop.

I was astonished to learn the celebrity visitor would be none other than Michael Jordan. Turns out he was a huge fan of motorsports including 500cc motorcycle racing and F1. Talk about a perfect alignment of the planets. Here I was in France covering the achievements of a champion Australian motorcyclist and about to meet the undisputed master of a sport to which I devoted equal measures of attention. And just to think I had long harboured a belief that I must have been the only person on the planet with competing interests in basketball and motor racing!

Le Mans was a two hour drive southwest of Paris via the A11 and here I was chauffeuring the head of the Suzuki motorcycle team. What a scoop!

When we arrived at the famous circuit, I could see a black Hummer in the distance and guessed correctly it was the great man. His entourage included Ahmad Rashad, the ex-NFL player who was the famous court announcer at the United Centre. I suppose the helmets worn by American football players conspire against instant recognition so he was quite chuffed when I introduced myself and asked if he was Ahmad Rashad. He seemed very impressed, and I congratulated him on the great job he'd done in becoming synonymous with the tremendous atmosphere at the Bulls' cauldron. The United Centre was famous for its heavy atmosphere and big game build-up, featuring the suspenseful *Sirius* theme song composed by The Alan Parsons Project. That was always followed by the familiar huddle of the players when MJ would scream: "*What time is it?*" To which they all replied: "*Game Time!*" After complimenting Ahmad Rashad, I asked if it would be possible to have a photo taken with Michael, who by this stage had been mobbed by the starstruck members of the Suzuki team. Ahmad cut through the heaving room with his inimitable dulcet tones:

"Michael! Photograph!" After a few minutes Michael wandered over and shook my hand before posing for the pic. We chatted for about a minute, and I expressed surprise at his passion for 500cc motorcycles. He mentioned he loved riding the machines but mentioned the Bulls and his insurance company were not so keen on his need for speed.

What a thrill. My arm must have been bruised for a week from pinching myself. I had just met the greatest basketballer of all time and without any argument – at that precise moment – *the* most famous man on the planet. I was a very long way from Fairfield!

For the record – here is the Frank Vincent dream team of all time. Michael Jordan, Shaquille O'Neal, Dennis Rodman, Larry Bird, Magic Johnson and Wilt Chamberlain. In the land of the giants – these six in my view – tower above the rest.

CHAPTER 13

THE ROMANTIC RAT

You must be wondering by now how I managed to squeeze a love life into such a crammed schedule in chasing my career dreams.

The perpetual fatigue guaranteed by a daily 3am rising for a breakfast shift – and the vampire hours of the midnight to dawn roster, international time zones, the actual fatigue of long flights and the accompanying insomnia doesn't exactly add up to a cookie cutter husband.

But none of the above did little to disqualify me from the affections of a beautiful nurse I met through my brother when she collected her car from the panel beating workshop of the family business. Then we kept bumping into each other in and around the building where I worked and she worked-out every day at Bondi Junction. Our constant collisions were serendipitous, I thought, and couldn't be ignored.

I was smitten with this stunning, tall blonde but the pursuit of Victoria Munro would prove to be a major challenge. She was playing hard to get, and the harder she played the more determined I was to succeed in wooing this beauty from Sydney's eastern suburbs. I have to say my job at Triple M went a long way towards impressing her, and I enhanced my chances by showering her with free tickets to the concerts of big name acts and records and CDs that came my way. My biggest hurdle initially was Victoria's commitment to a recent boyfriend she left behind in the Middle East. She promised she would wait a year before she would be with another man and was a woman of her word.

Once I convinced Victoria that a woman shouldn't have to be beholden to such misogynistic demands our fledgling relationship blossomed into a full blown romance, and we started sharing her apartment in New South Head Rd.

Life was good. Victoria and I shared the same sense of humour and we made for a very happy couple. Four years later we were married in Balmain. It was a fantastic day and I had every reason to believe it would be plain sailing towards life as a family man. But my fluctuating fortunes at Triple M would end up having an impact on our relationship, and Victoria decided to delay having children. I was shattered but struggling to keep her happy as work troubles dogged my daily existence after my great mate and former 2SM jock Ian Grace was replaced as the station's program director. His replacement didn't rate me and life became a tortuous game of second guessing the new boss' moods and what seemed to be his capricious, unreasonable demands.

Ian Grace – a former star announcer and programmer hailing from 2SM – had left the Ms to run the radio arm of Richard Branson's burgeoning Virgin empire. Ian remains one of my closest and most supportive friends. I've lost count of the times Gracie has been there for me, to give me a reference or a long comforting chat. He is a champion par excellence. In my humble opinion Gracie was the doyen of programmers. He was a PD well known for going out to see bands live in getting a feel from the coalface on how the audience reactions would work to the same music played out of their home stereos and car speakers. Gracie was dedicated to his craft, and long before arriving at Triple M to grace the place (no pun intended) with his intuition and intelligence the very same qualities had worked wonders for 2SM's famous *Rock of the 80s* format, which had played a huge part in the top rating AM station's success before

Triple M arrived to steal the show – and go one better with its eclectic line-up of edgy announcers. As an excellent jock in his own right Gracie's empathy with announcers was second to none, and even the biggest of egos would have to respect the authority of a colleague who had walked the walk and talked the talk.

If Gracie had stayed at the Ms I'm sure fate would have dealt me a kinder hand, but as it happened my nemesis at the Ms at one stage even fired me after I blew-up over my place on the roster for floating announcers. They rehired me immediately after tempers cooled down, but the writing was on the wall. I felt like I was in the crosshairs and the stress was manifesting in tension at home. Victoria became increasingly distant, and I seemed powerless to win her back. After admitting she wasn't certain about whether her future was lying with me after all I tried everything to reignite our romance, but her head and heart appeared to be elsewhere. When she eventually left the new home I had bought in Leichhardt something died inside me and it never came back. I was heartbroken.

I found myself working in the Pyrmont media centre for the Sydney 2000 games, a job that would lead to my employment by the international outside broadcast company Host Broadcast Services, which had also been contracted to provide high end production facilities for the 2002 World Cup in Seoul and Tokyo. They had been impressed by the way operated during the Sydney Games and offered me a gig in production liaison for my very first job at a World Cup. I was over the moon but would have been more excited to know this assignment would fill the big hole in my soul after the demise of my marriage to Victoria and a subsequent relationship that also failed.

My second chance at real love arrived in the delightful form of Miki Matsukawa – a Japanese employee of HBS based in Tokyo. At first Miki was playing it cool, ignoring my phone calls and taking forever to return them. But I was falling in love. This beautiful woman from Toyko was suddenly reappearing in my life when I travelled to Amsterdam to attend a reunion party for the HBS' World Cup team. Miki admitted she had missed me and so began a wonderful relationship. I would live in Holland for another 10 years, returning to Australia to get married. For 18 years Miki would be my best friend.

We shared wonderful times, including a trip to Zanzibar after Miki decided it would be somewhere novel and exotic. I wasn't convinced but was stunned to learn most of the locals could not give us directions to the childhood home of Rock God Freddie Mercury. We finally found it after a waitress consulted the kitchen and one of the chefs revealed it was in an apartment building about 20 metres away. And there it was – with a small sign of the door confirming it, untouched by vandals and left alone by thieves who would otherwise fetch a fair price for this rare piece of rock 'n' roll memorabilia.

After leaving Amsterdam Miki and I lived in Canberra before settling in the Queensland resort town of Noosa. But with my radical hours and her frequent and increasingly longer overseas assignments the sun wasn't always shining on our little corner of the Sunshine Coast, and it would eventually set for us, never to rise again. The geographical separation inevitably became an unbridgeable emotional distance, and we'd go our separate ways for the final time.

CHAPTER 14

THE WORLD GAME

When I read all about the record ratings of the World Cup on SBS and see sell-out crowds at Australian stadiums hosting friendlies between local teams and the star-studded sides of the English Premier League I can't help but think back to the days when the very mention of the word 'soccer' would symbolise the racism and bigotry that prevailed in Sydney's hostile suburbs.

It was clear to me from a young age that Australia's idea of 'football' was confined to the oval, variety, used in both Rugby codes and what was then known as Australian Rules.

As a student at a high school that had Rugby League as a core part of its mission statement 'wog ball' as it was known – was the most unfashionable of all four codes. It was seen as the sport of ethnic minorities, and somehow characterised as 'soft' in the absence of death defying spear tackles, bone ratting shoulder charges and stiff arms to the head. Try telling the hard heads of northern England that soccer is a 'sissy's game' and see what happens at the bar of a Manchester boozer!

In canvassing many theories for why Australia was slow to embrace the World Game I thought at one stage that maybe our original status as a penal colony – and subsequent distaste for anything to do with 'Poms' – especially their cricket team – had sparked a visceral rebellious response to the idea we should embrace the national past time of the United Kingdom. Although just as quickly the popularity of cricket in Australia undermined my theory. Maybe it had nothing to do with the mother country at all – and the sport had simply become a lightning rod for the racism that lingered here after the second world war – and Italians in particular were playing for the 'wrong side' then!

With my good friend and Triple M afternoon announcer Ron E Sparx sharing bubbles with American football megastar Joe Montana, in Sydney for NBC after Sydney won the rights for the 2000 Olympic Games.

I spent 12 years in Europe trying to learn as much as possible about football. Thankfully SBS recognised my commitment to the game by feeding me as much work as possible. My story suggestions were always welcomed with open arms.

The fact soccer is The World Game has finally been embraced by Australians. I guess the seeds were sewn way back in 1974 when the Socceroos qualified for the World Cup. Thanks to Gough Whitlam our multicultural mix was renewed, and new generations of players and supporters emerged to the point where one of our national Broadcasters SBS took on football as the central plank of its sporting coverage.

This gave Australians of all backgrounds their first opportunity to see quality games from every corner of the globe. Until then Australian TV coverage had been limited highlights package late on a Monday, capturing the previous week's English first division games in a program known as the big match. The only opportunity to see a world class meant getting up in the middle of the night to watch a grainy black and white satellite telecast of the FA Cup final.

I loved my job at Host Broadcast Services, guaranteeing my dress circle seats at five FIFA World Cups and a golden chance to see the world's greatest footballers.

With SBS committing so seriously to coverage of the World Game it was given new prominence, and its following continued to build to the point where our female national team the Matildas now commands plenty of attention.

SBS was always quick to scoop-up my suggestions for football feature stories such as Falkirk FC in Scotland which had four Australians on its roster. When I turned up to Falkirk training the week before their Scottish cup match against Glasgow Rangers, the atmosphere in the camp was noticeably confident. I was also taken away by the exact location of the training camp. I had a Mel Gibson moment when I realised the Falkirk training camp was in the shadows of the William Wallace memorial, noticeably further up the hill of Sterling. Coach John Hughes couldn't do enough for me and the Australian players were all willing to be interviewed. I was so confident they would beat the Rangers in that Scottish cup match that I went to Ladbroke's betting shop to back them. I wrote on the betting ticket, "Falkirk, absolute special to beat Rangers." The person taking the bet asked me to clarify what I meant by this, asking “does this mean you want to back Falkirk?” He then told me the odds of Falkirk were 5/1 and I immediately placed 50 pounds on the team. A win of 250 pounds!

With the likes of Brett Emerton, Mark Viduka and Tim Cahill becoming EPL superstars and further successful qualification campaigns Australian soccer was finally starting to receive the attention it deserved all along. Speaking of Emerton and Viduka reminds of when young English striker Alan Smith moved from Leeds to Manchester United and pulled me aside while I was conducting post-match interviews. He asked if I was Australian, because he wanted to reveal his disappointment over the retirement Newcastle Rugby League immortal Andrew Johns – who’d been the brightest of shining stars on Kangaroo tours of England. I was amazed to think an English footballer of such standing would be in awe of an Aussie legend from a rival code, but then canvassed the real possibility that Smith had grown in the sort of family in Northern England where league was very popular with the working class. I went on to follow his career with Man U, Newcastle and as he capped in the English team on 19 occasions between 2001 and 2009.

To deepen one’s appreciation of just how far the game has come down under since the days I was forced to defend my participation, you only have to look at the superstardom of Chelsea’s Aussie striker Sam Kerr. Way before Sam’s emergence on the world stage the advancement of the women’s game was making itself glaringly apparent to me when I witnessed one Matilda hit the crossbar after striking the ball with her right foot before using her left to slam it into the back of the net. Soccer in Australia was literally scoring goals with both feet!

Journalists are not known for being gracious is recognising one another's talents and contributions, but if that's some sort of rule I'd like to be the conspicuous exception in delivering high praise to the late SBS TV legend Les Murray. The Hungarian born soccer scribe in my view has done more than any other Australian to elevate the World Game in this country to prominence it should always have commanded.

But his untiring efforts to promote a sport would also go so much further in tightening the knit of Australia's multi-cultural society. Attracting viewers to SBS's coverage might be judged by as incidental when compared with the net effect of raising the levels of national harmony. Just as sport can divide along tribal lines it can unite and anyone of the millions with an ethnic heritage in Australian can consider themselves indebted to László Ürge, Les' birth name – as he was known when growing up on Wollongong after his family arrived down under in 1957. Les was 12 then and his accent had been well and truly established before going on to become one of the most recognisable voices on the Australian air waves. The sheer force of his nature meant that a trip via the Max Roley School of Voice would be superfluous. He started at SBS in 1980 as a subtitler for Hungarian programs after changing his name while working as a relatively unknown commentator for Channel TEN in 1977.

Within six years of starting at SBS he was hosting the coverage of the 1986 World Cup and his name would become synonymous with the telecast right up until his death in 2017.

Les was given a State funeral, an honour also bestowed upon his partner in arms for promoting soccer – the late Socceroo Johnny Warren, who once famously said: "I want Australia to embrace this fabulous game. It's not wog-ball, this is the game of the world."

I didn't need to hear Johnny Warren's clarion call to embark upon my own mission to promote soccer, but it played a large part in inspiring me to become heavily involved in the television production of the 2002 FIFA World Cup. Les and Johnny were trail blazers in the true sense of that expression, using their pure passion to wake all Australians up to the power, precision and beauty of a sport that was adored in every other corner of the planet.

The relationship I forged with Host Broadcast Services would become a life changing association with profound professional and personal impacts that endure until this day.

The senior producers at HBS had been impressed particularly with the small part I played in directing camera operators on how they could frame the most effective shots. This experience in Sydney led to a direction from HBS to work at the 2002 FIFA World Cup hosted by Japan and Korea, where I would be based in Seoul for eight months.

On one occasion I joined a large number of colleagues on their trip to the Demilitarised Zone (DMZ). I was alarmed by how close Seoul is to the danger zone. Less than 90 minutes north of the capital the first of many heavily guarded bunkers appeared, soon followed by large squadrons of Korean soldiers posted with tanks and artillery. The DMZ itself was extremely surreal. A one kilometre stretch of vacant land, heavily guarded on both sides. Guards posted on both sides discouraged the use of cameras of any description. The next night I was drinking at a popular marine hangout, the Iguana bar. I was talking to one marine and he told me his job was to stand on the line of the South Korean side. The face of a North Korean soldier standing directly opposite from him was quite visible. When I asked what his attitude towards that soldier was, he replied "I can't wait to kill him." Another interesting experience was my conversation with one of my assistants, a 22 year old university student, when I asked "why do Koreans hate the Japanese so much." She immediately replied: "They fucked our mothers."

I was one of the few people not wearing Manchester United merchandise at that tournament. Having become a Chelsea fan by then, I proudly wore their blue colours almost every time I ventured out into public.

Australia-based senior HBS production manager Garry Shaw had noticed that unlike the hordes of fans jumping on the bandwagon of Manchester United's enormous global popularity, I could be seen wearing a Blues jumper. He assumed correctly that I was serious football fan – and had no doubt my understanding of the sport would be intimate enough to succeed in the role of a Senior Broadcast Liaison Officer.

My career was shifting dramatically from behind the microphone, drawing upon all my years of broadcasting experience as a sports journalist. With my participation in the coverage two Olympic Games, NBA finals and world motor racing championships already under my belt the progression to working on the biggest sporting show on earth seemed natural enough.

My understanding of the needs of broadcasters was intimate, and HBS considered me an almost obvious selection for the leading liaison role, with my capacity to recognise potential challenges and address them before they became a problem. It's unsung but vital work. I went from being a cog in the coverage machine to providing the oil for its seamless operation – taken for granted by viewers as they reach for the remote to expect the stream of first class coverage to be as reliable as any water pouring from a tap.

The electronic plumbing of television sport coverage in the emerging digital age was complicated to say the least, and I was expected to have quick solutions for any glitches involving anything from the endless reels of cabling and wiring to where a commentator should be standing for his sideline analysis. I was the HBS go-to-man for broadcasters needing answers in a big hurry.

The Koreans and Japanese were already leading the world in the mass production of electronics and motor vehicles when I arrived at the FIFA International Broadcast Centre in Seoul to discover this world cup would indeed benefit from the technology already developed by the two most sophisticated economies of democratic Asia.

Both nations were going above and beyond to ensure this event would be the most modern and efficient in its history, and they succeeded spectacularly. The stadiums were magnificent, and the streets were buzzing with a large dose of world cup fever. In two countries where baseball was the national past time soccer was making a noisy if not belated arrival, but not celebrated enough according to South Korea's legendary coach Guus Hiddink, who berated the local's media's ongoing obsession with the bats and balls of the summer sport. Hiddink's confidence was substantiated by the on field performance of South Korea. This was clearly displayed one day after a training session of South Korea during an impromptu press conference when the prime minister phoned him at an inconvenient time. Hiddink asked the prime minister to call back later because he was too busy.

Hiddink would end up demanding attention with the incredible performance of the host side, reaching the semi-finals against all the odds only to be denied by German midfielder Michael Ballack. He was playing the dual roles of hero and villain as South Korea declared a national holiday for the game in the hope the local underdogs could emulate their earlier David v Goliath feats in defeating tournament juggernauts Portugal, Italy and Spain.

But Ballack would be the nemesis of the Koreans in every respect. As seven million singing and dancing fans crowded into city squares across the country Ballack put Germany ahead one nil, before emerging in the second half to cut down striker Lee Chun-soo as the Korean zeroed in on the goal. The automatic one match ban from the German's second yellow card of the tournament could well have been the deciding factor as Brazil won the final to become the first team to win five World Cup titles. Two second half goals from Ronaldo secured the victory and snared the Golden Shoe Award with his eight goals for the tournament.

As the Brazilians celebrated and my spirits were soaring for very personal reasons, after meeting the Toyko woman who would go on to become the great love of my life, but I hadn't put the 'ball in the net' just yet....

One victory of which I could be assured however was my permanent place on the Host Broadcast Services team, and four years later I was re-joining the crew to play the same liaison role for the 2006 FIFA World Cup in Germany.

At the time the German league was arguably the best in Europe, and the atmosphere of this tournament would be markedly different from the spirit of the Asian World Cup.

In my experience it's hard to compete with the passions of World Cup when it's staged by a football loving nation. There was no baseball, cricket, Rugby or any sport to rival soccer as the entrenched national sport of Germany.

German spectators for example would not burst into wild applause for the simple act of a throw in. This was a highly educated cohort of sophisticated fans, ready to clap in appreciation of the game's more subtle arts, and ruthlessly express their dissatisfaction for any play lacking imagination. The efficiency one would expect from the modern powerhouse of the European economy didn't however translate to success on the pitch for the host team. Germany finished third in the tournament, and Italy would snare the cup on penalties after finishing 1–1 with France at fulltime in the final. As a journalist of Italian descent, who could understand my mother tongue without being able to speak it fluently, I was nonetheless emotionally moved by Italy's win, and for a few days at least *Francesco Vincenzo Movizio* was making a big comeback in the thick of celebrations by my ancestral compatriots!

I loved that trip to Germany. Berlin was amazing, and I was particularly fond of Hamburg, the setting for so much musical history with the venues that hosted The Beatles in their early days. The most famous of these haunts was the Star Club, which also boasted performances from the likes of Ray Charles, Bo Diddley, Bill Hayley, Jimi Hendrix, Black Sabbath, Cream and Little Richard. Sadly the Star Club is now a hamburger joint.

Contrary to what the British would have the world believe I found the Germans to be very warm, intelligent, and accommodating – with a great sense of humour. They were fantastic hosts, and 2006 remains one of my most satisfying World Cup experiences, and not just because of the heroics produced by The Azzurri!

The next world Cup would take me to South Africa, hosting its first international sporting event since the end of Apartheid. But the celebration of the occasion would be drowned out by an instrument that was destined to destroy the enjoyment of the competition for millions.

The infamous vuvuzela – a single noted horn that could send people deaf, mad or both – in the hands of the thousands that packed South Africa's stadiums, and made life hell for the players, commentators and the world-wide television audience. FIFA failed to act in restricting their use, defending the instrument as an integral part of local culture. The racket they created from dawn until dusk deprived players of sleep, and made vital on field communication next to impossible.

The noise was variously described as anything akin to a herd of 'irate elephants' to 'a swarm of wasps', amplified to decibels that could cause physical harm to the hearing of those forced to suffer the unrelenting cacophony. It seemed such a shame. South Africa had waited an eternity for its time in the global sun, and the World Cup was being sabotaged by the ubiquitous, maddening vuvuzelas.

Dany Levy from the Sport Blog summed it up "Whoever thought the end of the world might come from a long plastic horn?"

The San Francisco Chronicle's Bruce Jenkins was chillingly accurate in his prediction of what amounted to a disaster: "Given a golden opportunity to ban vuvuzelas, those pathetic and annoying air-horns being passed off as musical instruments, FIFA declared them 'part of South Africa's soccer culture' and has refused to ban them for the event, which begins Friday. Thousands of miles away, we will all be suffering over such blatant disregard for common sense."

Spanish musicologist Pedro Espi-Sanchis weighed in: "On television all you can hear is those rhythms mixing into a grey drone of the B-flat and that's what millions of people will be hearing during this World Cup. That is really what hurt me as a musician ... that is not Africa."

Some websites were stampeded by millions looking for end to the suffering in their living rooms. The makers of a $3.50 anti-vuvuzela filter instructed users to play their downloadable MP3 alongside their TVs speakers, promising: "the resulting soundwave may be so faint as to be inaudible to human ears." Critics said this so-called solution only served to make the problem twice as bad.

Others advised the masses to adjust TV's sound settings by reducing the treble to zero and literally tone down the most annoying 'buzzsaw-in-the-brain' frequencies.

Players were furious. France captain Patrice Evra blamed the horn on the fatigue of his teammates.

"We can't sleep at night because of the vuvuzelas. People start playing them from 6am," he said.

"We can't hear one another out on the pitch because of them."

Portuguese superstar Cristiano Ronaldo joined the chorus of condemnation before surrendering to the inevitability of the ongoing pain, in the face of FIFA's adamant refusal to ban the plastic horns.

"It is difficult for anyone on the pitch to concentrate," the Portugal star told a press conference.

"A lot of players don't like them, but they are going to have to get used to them."

There could be no doubt the Spaniards succeeded more than any other team in maintaining their concentration, prevailing over the Netherlands 1–0 in the final.

After the BBC switchboard melted down and joined other broadcasters in offering an alternative channel with minimised vuvuzela noise FIFA eventually stopped turning its own deaf years and banned the use of any musical instruments in the arenas of the following World Cup in Brazil.

I wasn't prepared to rely on crude plastic replicas of a South African cultural icon to get my own taste of real life there. The World Cup has taught me as much about humanity as it has in acquainting me with elite sport at its highest level. I always made a point of hitting the streets of whatever country I visited in my many travels. I hired a car in South Africa for a road trip to predominantly indigenous Pretoria to sample the true nature of this nation in the wake of its oppressive past.

While the big cites of South Africa were impressive enough there was plenty of lingering evidence from a disgraceful era that ensured a huge, unassailable gulf between the haves and the have nots.

At one point on my journey, I was stopped by a young man who was hitchhiking along the highway on a mission to find water and money.

I immediately offered him four big bottles of water I had in the car, and then emptied coins out a small compartment in the dash amounting to about $20. I asked the young bloke how far he had to walk. He said he had already walked five kilometres and had another five to go. It was a sobering moment of reflecting on the great fortune to have been born in country such as Australia, where water and an abundance of so much more provides a dramatic contrast to life for so many wretched millions in other countries. I've always been keen to preserve water, taught to turn the taps off until it's time to rinse my toothbrush and minimising the amount needed for washing the dishes was compulsory in the Movizio household. Nothing irks me more than seeing Australians mucking around with ice baths in social media postings. Each time I witness such antics I recall that kid who would have walked 20 kilometres just to buy a bottle of water while trying his luck in the pursuit of a random stranger's spare change. As I approached the Pretoria Stadium I couldn't help but be troubled when juxtaposing the mouth-watering $400 million spent on its renovation with the poverty of those wretched thousands who battled with day-to-day poverty while somehow managing to exist in its imposing shadows.

There was nothing FIFA could do to prevent music and dancing on the streets of Rio when its four yearly extravaganzas arrived in

Brazil in 2014. Legendary for its carnival atmosphere Brazil was an idyllic celebratory setting for football's version of Disneyland, even if the infrastructure for the event was sadly wanting for completion.

To justify the enormous cost of construction the Brazilian Government vowed to reinvent the stadia as prisons after the World Cup, and many of the arenas – while impressive at first glance – were still in a sad state by the time our HBS team arrived a week before kick-off. There were grandstand seats still covered in plastic and the construction authority had all but abandoned any attempts to dress-up the precincts of some arenas with landscaping.

With 111 days to go before the opening ceremony four of the 12 stadiums were unfinished after the final deadline had passed two months earlier. Arguments raged about who should pick up the bill for temporary stands earmarked for some of the stadiums as ticket demand continue to build strongly.

The budget concerns and claims of corruption in the disrupted preparations had already led to a massive public backlash, with hundreds of thousands taking to streets to oppose the reckless use of so much public funding. One survey claimed 61 percent of Brazilians would have preferred the $13 billion funding to be directed towards vitally needed public services.

Public transport was also wanting after several big cities scrapped plans for extra bus lanes and light rail lines. Only 10 of the 56 infrastructure projects promised for the event were finished. Ten days before the tournament finished an overpass under construction in Belo Horizonte collapsed, killing two people and injuring 22 others on the carriageway below.

The Brazilian Government found a strong supporter in 2002 World Cup hero and organising committee member Ronaldo who insisted: "The World Cup is big business for the country and we have to show the tiny minority that is against the tournament that it is going to leave a legacy for our nation."

But the facilities were seriously underdone. The cameras didn't really tell the story of the shoddy construction standards. It wound my memory back to Seoul and Tokyo and how the new infrastructure of those city's would still have put Brazil's effort to shame, even from 14 years after the Asian tournament. But I couldn't really complain. I always had the best seats in the house, often occupying glassed-in studios to watch the games after the various TV hosts had moved to other parts of the stand!

As quickly as Brazil could disappoint it could just as easily take your breath away. The beaches of the northern regions were postcard perfect and Rio itself would have to be the most stunning city on the planet. Its beauty is bordering on surreal, sealed by the sublime spectacle of the illuminated Cristo Redentor (Christ the Redeemer) statue, set against the night sky on at the summit of the 700 metre Corcovado Mountain.

Millions of fans were certainly looking to the summit for spiritual comfort after the Germans trounced Brazil 7–1 before defeating Argentina 1–nil in the final.

Although the 2018 World Cup was staged in the warmer months, I always imagined Russia to be cold after the movies Dr Zhivago and Gorky Park must have been frozen into my sub conscious.

The weather was in fact beautiful but my reception in the western city of Kaliningrad was frosty to say the very least after two police officers singled me out for interrogation when our bus pulled-up at the HBS Hotel. My sin? I was wearing a Wests Tigers NRL jumper, and they thought I was some kind of hooligan. It took some fast talking from a Russian speaking colleague from Belarus to calm the cops down, and they retreated altogether once I finally produced my accreditation. But it was an unpleasant way to start my latest cup campaign and at odds with the perception I went on to form about the warmth of the Russian people. The brush with the constabulary was wiped by my encounter with a stranger at a train station who offered to help with my luggage.

I found Russia to be fascinating and was mightily impressed by the high standard of the facilities. The stadium where I was based played host to a block buster between Belgium and England, a game the English were suspected of throwing to give their opponents a harder draw before the finals.

The highlights of the Russia trip included a visit to the magnificent Krestovsky Stadium in St Petersburg, the 68,000 seater home of the Roman Abramovic owned Zenit side.

Moscow was also wonderful, a thoroughly modern city – again removed from subliminal clichés embedded no doubt by years of seeing the city's portrayal in the movies – including Gorky Park – which meant I had to go there and see what all the fuss had been about. Far from feeling like I had stepped onto the set of a spy thriller I felt very comfortable at Gorky Park, and was impressed with its lively restaurant, bars and nightlife.

As you'd expect I also made it to Moscow's Luzhniki Stadium, where France would defeat Croatia 4–2 in the final to complete my fifth and final World Cup tour, having been paid for the privilege all along!

CHAPTER 15

AMSTERDAM

Falling in love with Miki Matsukawa meant moving to Amsterdam in 2004 and living what I considered to be the ten happiest years of my life.

The lure of a beautiful woman and a magnificent city proved to be irresistible.

And as if life were not perfect enough, I was soon able to again indulge my passion for broadcasting. Securing a working visa for just a few hundred Euro I started knocking on doors and before long one flew open, and I began work as an announcer on English Breakfast Radio – an online enterprise that also presented the opportunities to show video, a novel combination at the time, requiring the use of emerging digital camera technology still six years away from the introduction of the first iPhone.

Contemplating the grand scheme of things and wondering whether I would raid another chocolate shop in the historic Belgian city of Bruges.

I was living in Miki's flat in the heart of what you would call picture postcard Amsterdam, overlooking the world heritage listed Prinsengracht, a three kilometre long canal named after the Prince of Orange when it was built way back in 1612. We would walk along this waterway every day while pinching ourselves about our incredibly good fortune. The canal is considered Amsterdam's finest, lined with churches, museums, and cafes. On weekends we'd join hands for the walk to an organic farmers' market at Noordermarkt square, where we'd find fresh flowers, herring, pickles, and other delicacies. Miki and I never felt luckier than the constant reminder that we had each other. She was such a sweetheart, working tirelessly to make our home a perfect nest.

We were so fond of Prinsengracht we renamed it Onzengracht *(our canal)* and made a pact to kiss every time we walked it. I remember holding up traffic one day when dismounting our bicycles to kiss on the edge of Onzengracht – so well received that it was even applauded by those who witnessed it!

Amsterdam had become the 'set' for the 'movie of our romance.'

We had our other favourite films of course, including *In Bruges*, a very clever black comedy starring Colin Farrell, set in the Belgian city of Bruges. We liked the film so much Miki arranged a work trip to Bruges, a 250 km drive to the south of Amsterdam. We had a wonderful time exploring its rich history, dating back to the days of Julius Caesar's conquest of the Menapii Belgian tribes in the 1st century BC! So, it's a bit older than The Rocks in Sydney!

I absolutely loved losing myself in the heritage of these ancient lands – but not as much as the chocolate shops of Bruges. Yum. The caramel centred cubes of Dumon are to die for!

Amsterdam also has a big history for a city of just 900,000 people and was once the most influential commercial centre in the world as the sea-faring Dutch reaped the rich rewards of colonisation in the 17th and 18th centuries. The Dutch East India shipping line had guaranteed Amsterdam's future as one of the world's most liveable, dynamic cities, ranked number 9 in more recent surveys.

Its economy receives a major boost from tourism to the extent locals are constantly resisting the unrelenting influx to prevent the capital from becoming inundated in the same way Venice's canals have left the Italian city struggling to deal with its immense popularity. When the core of a famous city with so many canals become larger than life itself the logistics of dealing with tides of tourists become more formidable than the actual tidal impacts on infrastructure and services. But the Dutch manage to defy such pressures in maintaining a famously friendly disposition, and they're always ready to switch their speaking to English when sensing someone who struggles with their rudimentary Dutch – and that courtesy was always extended to yours truly.

Between Miki's Japanese and the Dutch spoken by everybody else I guess I could have become trilingual but in landing a gig at English Breakfast Radio those language skills simply weren't needed.

I was entering a Golden Age of my career, landing back behind a microphone and about to seize an opportunity for resuming my deep connection to the coverage of football.

Dutch based media company Endemol was looking for an English speaking football commentator. Better known for its reality TV franchises such as Big Brother and Deal or No Deal, Endemol had won the right for the coverage of *The Eredivisie*, the top tier of professional football in the Netherlands, founded in 1956, and ranked by UEFA as the sixth best league in Europe after Spain, Germany, England, France and Italy.

Of the 18 professional football clubs in The Netherlands Ajax is the most successful, winning 36 titles and finishing runner-up 23 times since the Eredivisie was formed in 1956. The biggest challenge confronting me in the new job was mastering the correct pronunciation of player names.

Amsterdam also became my base for covering the English Premier League as a freelancer for Australia's SBS – and of course my launch pad for heading to those World Cups in Germany and South Africa. Soccer had become my life.

I absolutely cherished my many journeys across the channel to cover the EPL at a time when my team Chelsea was dominating the league with back to back titles under the enigmatic Jose Mourinho. I interviewed Mourinho after a preseason friendly between Chelsea and Feyenoord in Rotterdam where he happily stopped and spoke to me without any booking.

I had access-all-areas media accreditation from the EPL and visited the dressing rooms of the biggest clubs in the land for the pre and post-match interviews. The highlights included a chat with superstar Chelsea striker Didier Drogba. Responding to my Australian accent he initially responded by saying "looooooong waaaaaaay!" But Didier was fantastic, giving me exactly what I needed. Later as I was leaving Stamford Bridge I could hear the noises of a loud, celebratory gathering coming from the bottom of the stand near the players and staff carpark. Suddenly Drogba's face appeared and he pointed at me. "Kangaroo!" he yelled, with a big smile of course.

Not all the players were friendly though. I remember a prickly Aussie EPL player giving me a flat out refusal to be interviewed after he'd made a name for himself with Leeds and Liverpool. I approached Harry Kewell him on the basis that we'd grown up in the same western Sydney neighbourhood, but not even that coincidence was enough to stop him from walking off after he simply gave me a blunt: "No." Charming!

Victorian striker Mark Viduka was much more accommodating. He had joined Kewell in leaving Leeds after that club's relegation.

At Britain's Silverstone race rack to interview a young Mark Webber, who would go on to become an Australian F1 superstar.

Viduka landed at Middlesbrough in 2004 and would end his English playing career at Newcastle United five years later. The big striker could not have been more obliging to deal with. Once he had spotted me from the Newcastle team bus, and immediately hopped off it to give me a few words. On another occasion an overzealous Football Federation Australia PR person tried to stop us from having a casual chat – and Mark quickly interjected. "It's alright.... he's ok!"

One of my more special destinations for EPL coverage was Old Trafford, home of the mighty Manchester United. I once had a tremendously productive night conducting post- match interviews with the likes of Ryan Giggs, Michael Carrick, Alan Smith, Patrice Evra and Cristiano Ronaldo. This night was example of how backing yourself proved to be an enormous winner. Australian F1 driver Mark Webber made the half time raffle ticket draw on field. I walked up to him for a chat which ended in Mark joining me on a media box to view the second half of the match, won by Manchester United in a UEFA champions league record score of 7–1 against AS Roma.

If only the walls of this place could talk – or scream – like the time master coach Sir Alex Ferguson was berating the team and kicked a shoe into the forehead of mercurial midfielder David Beckham. He was way beyond a pretty face Beckham. He had technical ability to match his God-given Hollywood looks. Although he was probably forced to turn and chase once too often, he more than compensated for any defensive weaknesses with dead-eye accuracy. He could land a pass on a twenty cent piece and bend it of course! The ball seemed connected to his twinkle toes with a length of string.

An interview with Chelsea legend Frank Lampard was another outstanding moment in the UK, where you could always count on the crowds to give you a hearty laugh. I remember a huge group of Liverpool supporters striking up their version of the Reds anthem: *You'll Never Walk Alone* to which the Chelsea supporters responded in the same tune: '*You'll never have a job.*' Cruel but funny...

Another outstanding highlight among my hundreds of interviews with the stars of the EPL was the pleasure of meeting master coach Jose Mourinho. Contrary to the frosty, aloof image the English tabloids contrived for the man they cruelly dubbed 'The Special One' this gentle Portuguese man was a picture of perfect manners and obliged me not once but twice when I requested a few words on mic. When I stopped to ask him the first time if he would mind being interviewed by Australian TV he immediately agreed, without brushing me off to his media manager. At complete odds with his portrayal in the red top press Jose was thoughtful, intelligent, sensitive, articulate and a genuine scholar of the game, graduating of course with the honours of back-to-back flags with Chelsea in 2005 and 2006, before he repeated the feat upon his return to Chelsea in for the 2014–2015 season. I also interviewed the England World Cup coach Gareth Southgate when he was coaching Middlesboro. Halfway through the chat a player jumped on him – and far from angry – Gareth immediately showed his qualities as a good bloke, taking it in good humour and piggybacked the intruder around the field. It was a great laugh. The serious business of EPL wasn't always a stern-faced affair.

On top of my Dutch league broadcasting, my EPL coverage and trips to the World Cup I could also travel from Amsterdam with Miki to cover the UEFA Champions League in Paris. With the leading French club Paris St Germain, a constant fixture in the Champions League I could base myself at Le Parc de Prince in the 16th arrondissement, and get to see the local team play all the leading clubs of Europe. It was a great opportunity to watch the megastars in action for their clubs, away from their national duties at World cups. Lionel Messi, Cristiano Ronaldo, Neymar and Zlatan Ibrahimovic would all turn-up at various stages to take on PSG and my clever partner also spoke French, was with me to make my work in Paris run even more smoothly.

Back in Amsterdam tensions with the Muslim community were reaching fever pitch after the gruesome November 2004 murder of Dutch filmmaker Theo van Gogh. He was killed in broad daylight on a busy street by a 26-year-old Dutch citizen of Moroccan descent. He shot van Gogh, slit his throat, and pinned a five-page condemnation of Western society to the filmmaker's body.

The murder triggered a series of violent reactions, including a vicious brawl in a bar where Miki and I had been drinking with a friend. Fists were flying everywhere, and I feared knives or guns could be produced at any minute. The three of us fled. On the way out I stepped in a pool of blood. I later discovered my clothing was spattered with blood. It had been a blood bath. The episode was freakishly inconsistent with what had been the prevailing atmosphere of a peaceful and progressive city.

The next year London would be bombed in a series of terror attacks. September 11 and the Bali Bombings were still painfully fresh in everyone's mind, and now Amsterdam was literally in the firing line of extremists who had answered the clarion call to keep striking popular western targets. These were tense times, and they were about to become as anxious as they've ever been for me upon my eventual return to Australia in a disgraceful episode that turned my happy world upside down.

CHAPTER 16

VICIOUS AND VEXATIOUS

For anyone unfamiliar with the word *anathema* it means this: *something or someone one vehemently dislikes.*

After what I endured along with other children sent to Catholic schools, catalogued comprehensively in chapter three, I apply *anathema* to describe my feelings about any form of bullying or harassment. I witnessed and suffered too much of it to be anything other than passionate in my condemnation of such behaviour from those who choose to abuse their positions of authority and direct power. That's why I have rebelled against the cold blooded humanoids I have struck in management throughout my career, knowing these corporate sycophants will always prioritise the protection of their own backsides above those of any one under their charge. As former Prime Minister Paul Keating always enjoyed quoting from the late NSW Premier Jack Lang: "in the race of life always back self-interest – at least you know it's trying."

When push comes to shove these soulless arseholes will push, and shove anyone who challenges them right out the front door. I've lost count of the teams in which I've been a member that are forced to mutter and grumble under their breath and then smile disingenuously when having to deal with the less savoury consequences of taking our place in the corporate 'serfdom.' Woe beholds any robust free thinker who dares to take-on the shadow men bidding on behalf of those more interested in dollars than any moral profit to be found in a much more profound contribution to the improvement of the world as we know it.

I have always secretly envied the freedom and honesty of the self-employed such as tradies for the privilege of being able to run their own show. Sure, their worlds will intersect and clash with the larger companies and their bureaucracies – especially when contractors wait an eternity for invoices to be paid – but at the end of the day they can drive home and crack open a beer to quench a hard earned thirst, and never need alcohol to rinse their mouth from the grime of the backsides that are licked elsewhere. The arselickers were just like those prefects who deputised for the deviants of Patrician brothers. They were always ready to tell the bosses what they wanted to hear, in defiance of any inconvenient reality about the true state of affairs, like staff morale for example!

Calm before the storm, a 2CA publicity shot on the peaceful shores of Lake Burley Griffin.

I always took a leaf out of Doug Mulray's book in backing my own judgment and ability to tell the bosses what they didn't want to hear or know. Always one to call *a spade a shovel* I wasn't exactly popular with management for my unfiltered view of the world – an honesty others found confronting or resented – particularly if I literally shared my opinion with the wider world via that device commonly known as a microphone.

My stint with English Breakfast radio in Amsterdam was a constant reminder of how much I missed broadcasting back home.

I started sending recordings of my show back to Australia, and in 2014 a familiar stomping ground was beckoning. Radio 2CA Canberra was struggling and looking for a new brekky jock to lift the ratings from the basement. The opportunity carried all the promise of a major comeback and although the money was chicken feed I had saved enough over the years to compensate for 2CA management's meagre offering. They would pay me $300 for a shift that would extend from 5am until midday, almost the same pay I received 15 years earlier from the Canterbury Bankstown Bulldogs as the club's ground announcer for an afternoon's work every second Sunday.

I was quick enough to rationalise the poor renumeration. Just as Canberra had been a solid steppingstone in my career in the early 1980s I figured an encore 30 years later could relaunch me into the Sydney market. But as the saying goes: "make God laugh by telling him your plans."

With Miki staying in Amsterdam to continue her work with Nippon TV I found myself bracing again for Canberra's oven like summers and brutal winters, but the weather would never match the chill I was feeling from management just a few weeks into the job.

It was a promising enough beginning when my appointment was covered in the *Canberra City News* in November 2014.

FRANK Vincent, aka Uncle Frank, (aka The Black Rat), aka Franco Vincenzo Movizio, is returning home to host 2CA's Classic Breakfast show replacing fill in guy, Rob Duckworth.

Some may remember him as: Franko Vincenzo Movizio 'the inflatable sports reporter' on the Doug Mulray show or 'the reporter in the water with Wendy Harmer's Morning Crew, or the madcap rev-head on Network Ten's RPM program, during an illustrious career spanning 15 years in Australian radio and television.

Since moving to Europe more than a decade ago, Frank has gained quite a reputation for his offbeat sports commentaries. 'The Voice Of Dutch Football' is one tag he's been labelled with since accepting the role of play-by-play commentator on the Dutch Eredivisie competition, broadcast weekly to 15 countries on networks such as ESPN, Setanta Sports and Al Jazeera. Frank also talks European Football and UEFA Champions League weekly on the ABC's Grandstand Show, *voices AJAX TV's 60-minute international program and hosted the English Breakfast Radio Show on* 99.4FM *Amsterdam, with Francis Leach.*

Frank is no stranger to the Nation's Capital, having been part of 2CC's line up in the early 80's with his second tour of duty starting Monday November 3.

The local news story was accompanied by a photo of me standing on the shores of Lake Burley Griffin. I had arrived as a man with a plan to elevate the station's profile with a lively breakfast show that would echo the format of the most successful program in the history of Australian commercial radio. Having worked on the Doug Mulray show for so long in the 80s and 90s I had more than a fair idea of what would work in building a brand new audience in the national capital. If they laughed in Sydney they'd be laughing in Canberra, and we all know this place is always in need of lightening-up!

There's an art to a breakfast shift. You have to deliver a blast of positive energy to help the audience build momentum for a brand new day, right from the time listeners wake-up to their radio alarms. If you doubt that – consider the story of a breakfast announcer in the town of Young. He slept through his own alarm one morning, and suddenly most of the town was sleeping in. There were just crickets or what we call 'dead air' on their clock radio speakers, without any programming coming through in the days when stations in bush markets would automatically stop transmission between midnight and 5am. Unlike television there wasn't even a test transmission with muzak to make up for the absence of a live studio broadcast.

So having arrived in Canberra with a solid blueprint for succeeding, and 25 years of journalism under my belt in the three decades since my 1980s stint at 2CC I was confident of fulfilling my mission of improving the ratings for a perennial wooden spooner.

Not everyone was sharing my enthusiasm, and almost from the outset management was questioning my use of Uncle Frank as my nickname. They accused me of a straight lift from the Uncle Doug Mulray handle and argued that the station's demographic of baby boomers would not relate to how someone of their own era could be 'their uncle.' Don't get me wrong – as a creative I was well acquainted I with the traditional friction between management and the on air talent on which the bosses rely to improve their profits. Better ratings translate directly to more advertising dollars, but this symbiotic relationship is fraught at the best of times and just plain dreadful when they start telling the announcers how to do their jobs. I was far from shameless and proud to be using the Mulray Bunch as my inspiration for trying to replicate the success of the legendary Triple M breakfast show. It worked then – spectacularly and I was convinced a zany show, even without Doug, would make for compelling, entertaining radio to give this battling station on the AM band an even chance of building a bigger audience. But there's no doubt Mulray was a great mentor, and all these years later – still inspiring me.

Apart from the retrospective wisdom of the 'Monday morning quarterbacks' in management professional, rivalry is always another insidious force of negativity, and one's enemies within can always be relied upon to be busy white-anting any colleague they perceive as a threat to their own existence. Shortly after arriving at CA I caught out two other announcers bitching about the publicity I had received in that story about me as the *Man on the Street* for the Wendy Harmer show on 2Day FM.

I found the managers of 2CA to be a brutal bunch, loading their day-to-day advice with gratuitous expletives at a time when they could get away with aggressive behaviour. There was a constant stream of abuse usually punctuated with "fuck this, fuck that and fuck you!" For me this was an open invitation to say: "Get fucked!" When dealing with these legends in their own regional lunchtimes, I always made sure I gave as good as I got. Other staff would be genuinely intimidated, literally. They included one of my more timid colleagues, who once curled-up in the foetal position to cry after a blast from the those who ran the joint.

Many managers in radio mostly had a background in sales, and their swagger suggested that without the money they brought in nobody would be paid. I always believed they wouldn't be pulling in the bucks without the on-air talent to attract it. This was no 'chicken before the egg' scenario. These spivs with their gold identity bracelets had to have something to sell in the first place! In my case it was my name – a media personality who had spent more than 40 years building a bankable reputation, and I don't mean to convey any conceit in writing that, but such a perspective is much more economic than egotistical. By the age of 57 I had certainly forgotten more than the 2CA management had ever really known about broadcasting, and I was certainly old enough to use 'Uncle Frank' as my alter ego.

Ultimately the proof was in the pudding. Within three months I had taken 2CA's breakfast to midday ratings from 5.3% to 6.7%, helping the station to increase its 25–39 audience from 2.4% to 6.3% and more than double than number of listeners in the 40–54 demographic from 3.7% to 8% of the market. Even if the remuneration was lousy, I was rewarded somewhat with several promotional gimmicks, including my face on the back of local buses.

I would always point to the scoreboard whenever management started jumping on my balls, and they hated it. I was still being paid peanuts, and the relationship with the GM was beyond tense when he demanded I go above and beyond to give away chocolates for the sponsor of a Mother's Day promotion. I always stood my ground with management, and maybe this refusal to bend over led to those newspaper claims that I was 'untouchable.' It wasn't for the lack of any effort from management in trying to push me around!

My show meanwhile was powering. I was at the top of my game, and never felt more comfortable or confident on air. I was so bold that when an on air competition failed to attract a single listener phone call, I ended up interviewing myself, switching from my usual voice for the questions to an improvised yobbo accent for the answers. Then there were the celebrity interviews I secured. These superstars included KISS lead guitarist Ace Frehley, 60s icon Petula Clark and Nick Feldman from British pop sensation Wang Chung, famous for their smash hits *Dance Hall Days, Everybody Have Fun Tonight* and *Let's Go.* Feldman was a joy to host, and played along with my request to be addressed as Uncle Frank, referring to my new on air alter ego at least three times in the first 30 seconds of our chat.

Petula was a delight – 82 years young when we spoke about her glory days as the singer of the 1964 chartbuster *Downtown* and so many other hits.

She played right along when I would sing the opening line: "When you're alone and life is making you lonely You can always go....." and she would chime in with: "Downtown...." What a darling.

Without the support of a producer, I had the show cranking, and the audience kept growing to defy the increasing list of beefs management had been collecting on my on-air style. The air-conditioning in the corridors of 2CA was certainly much cooler than anything a savage Canberra winter was serving up outside. It didn't make any sense to me at all, but I couldn't help but feel management was the very incarnation of that adage that *success* has many fathers and failure was an *orphan*. The executives were queuing up to blow their own bags to the station's owners.

Throughout my on air career – from 2LT, to 2WL, 2CC, Triple M, 2DayFM and English Breakfast Radio there was a simple expectation for broadcasters to bring their A game to the studio. This was professional broadcasting, where there was no margin for glaring mistakes without repercussions and corrections. To stuff up once was unfortunate, but to paraphrase Oscar Wilde – to repeat the error was careless.

My 'crew' at 2CA amounted to myself and the news team. With three decades of reporting on my CV I certainly felt qualified to mentor the young reporters – and set them straight if I had to, if only for the sake of retaining the station's credibility. On one occasion I heard one of the news readers pronounce the surname of tennis legend John McEnroe as 'Mac-N-roe.' I pointed out that the 'en' in his name contained what's called a *neutral* or *indiscriminate* vowel sound in my efforts to ensure such a blunder wouldn't be repeated in future bulletins. I was to learn this episode, and others when I was forced to correct the presentation of the news – were to feature in a clandestine catalogue of what was later alleged to be my 'bullying behaviour.'

Suddenly my long career was colliding with a new era of sensitive petals. I was suddenly immersed in overly precious environment, minimising the priority of what once amounted to simple discipline and professionalism. I was hardly a Sergeant Major in my demeanour, far from it. I cared for these young journos and my empathy was guaranteed by very clear memories – and a lingering appreciation

– of the mentors who advised me along the way. I was a willing learner back in those days, and certainly not offended quickly by the simple, well-meaning act of providing valuable advice. The idea of running into management to complain about 'intimidation' was unthinkable, yet that's exactly what happened all these years later at 2CA as resentment grew about the professional standards I expected. Instead, this was scurrilously characterised as 'workplace bullying' and the very person making the complaint was soon changing her tune to complain that I had been 'overly friendly.' A trap was being set for the Black Rat, and management was using my news colleague as the 'cheese' it seemed.

The executive's determination to steal the glory for the station's resurgence had had them minimising my contribution, and I always sensed my days were numbered because of our uneasy relationship. What happened next confirmed my suspicions they would punt me at the first opportunity but there was no way I could have guessed the nastiness and ruthlessness they would employ in the process of what would become a very public and life shattering execution.

From the outset of this next story, I want to provide *context* in the form of my ultimate vindication, when I settled for a $50,000 payment of compensation from the publishers of *The Canberra Times* after the newspaper defamed me in the most horrendous way. That's

The stage was set for a triumphant return to the nation's capital, and it was a flying start before I went from the *back* of a bus to being *under it*.

how this story ends – or was supposed to end before the newspaper breached the conditions of the payout by neglecting to remove the online version of the completely unjustified vilification heaped upon me. That failure to uphold the compensation agreement and the indelible tattoo of Google would become the subject of further legal action.

So let me return to the seat of this vexatious inferno.

The same newsreader who had been mispronouncing John McEnroe's surname broke into tears one morning after driving all the way from Newcastle to Canberra only to discover she had not been rostered to work after all. This is how events unfolded, exactly as they happened, without any of the destructive ambiguity attached to the other party's eventual version of events.

The woman started crying after realising she had driven 450 kilometres in the dead of the night for nothing.

In the open space of a well-lit 'goldfish bowl' studio surrounded by big glass windows, with three other people in the building, I comforted her and we had what might be called a 'heart to heart' conversation that was personal on account of her own unsolicited disclosures. The talk ended with me reassuring her again and yes – I kissed her on the forehead. She then complained of being tense from the hard drive to Canberra and asked that I rub her shoulders. I obliged but at no stage did this physical contact manifest in any sexual way. I simply went back to work.

This episode was set against a backdrop of low morale among staff, including a few who claimed I could 'throw my weight around' because I was a 'management favourite.' Again, nothing could have been further from the truth, as I was to discover emphatically with the rudest awakening of my life.

I was literally asleep at home after a breakfast shift when the general manager called to reveal I'd been the subject of a harassment complaint by the same newsreader who had sought my comfort and confidence in her moment of distress.

To say I was flabbergasted would master the art of understatement. Of course, I was profuse with my denials and recounted the incident with the truth, without her subjective and pernicious embellishment.

By now I knew the sharks were starting to tighten their circle around me. They could smell my blood and humoured the journalist's 'concerns' by allowing her to read the news from another, smaller nearby studio. From that day onwards she would not acknowledge me, refusing to respond to the most basic greeting. It made for a very uncomfortable workplace environment, and I had a definite sense that even the most minor slip-up from me would result in my dismissal. The absence of any formal notice of my termination did nothing to remove the cold chill of the axe's blade from the back of my neck.

Fast forward six months and the Australian *#MeToo* movement was cranking-up after the bombshell revelations about notorious Hollywood sleazebag Harvey Weinstein. I watched as others including actor Kevin Spacey, comedian Louis CK and NBC anchor Matt Lauer were swept away in the same scandalous tsunami.

Then before long I was being contacted by *The Canberra Times* about the patently false claims about my conduct at 2CA. I was ordered by management not to respond – saying it would be in breach of contract they were about to tear-up in a matter of hours, but that didn't stop them from ordering not to defend myself publicly. They then sacked me after the newspaper breathlessly reported the following:

The company that controls Canberra radio station 2CA sacked breakfast presenter Frank Vincent on Tuesday after allegations of sexual harassment.

Mr Vincent was taken off the air a day after the board of Radio Canberra said it received a report from an independent investigator who was appointed last year to investigate harassment allegations.

The station has not disclosed any detail of the report, including its findings, but said the board had unanimously agreed to take immediate action after receiving it.

The sacking came the day after The Canberra Times put questions to the station's management about Mr Vincent's treatment of a junior journalist and other staff.

The subject of the investigation was sexual harassment. Other staff have made allegations about workplace culture and behaviour.

Station management is yet to answer the detailed questions provided this week.

Vincent began work at the station in November 2014 and remained on air until Tuesday morning.

He has strongly denied the allegations and said he was consulting lawyers.

A statement from Radio Canberra said, "Following allegations of harassment by an employee in the workplace, the board of Radio Canberra Pty Ltd directed management to engage an independent party to investigate the claims."

"The board received a copy of the independent investigator's report [on Monday] afternoon. Following receipt of this report, the directors unanimously agreed to take immediate action.

"Radio Canberra Pty Ltd has today terminated the employment of Frank Vincent with immediate effect.

"The directors of Radio Canberra Pty Ltd are committed to providing a safe workplace for all staff.

"The directors have determined to review current workplace policies and procedures and to implement training for all staff regarding their workplace rights."

Some interviews for the formal investigation were conducted in early 2017, and it is unclear why the report was only received by management on the same day as questions about Vincent.

A 2CA manager did not confirm who would replace Vincent on-air from Wednesday morning.

One of the more salacious mistruths of *The Canberra Times* coverage, quoted the journalist as saying:

"At first it was like working with an inappropriate uncle or someone who says things that are a little off, but you sort of shrug. It got progressively worse and I felt more and more uncomfortable.

"He would hug me pretty much every day when he got into work. This is 4 in the morning, there was no one else there... he would always hug me while I was sitting down so I'd be face to face with his crotch.

"When I told Michael Jones about what was going on with Frank, I feel like he didn't register the complaints as serious.

"Even though there was an investigation and they tried to get to the bottom of it, as soon as my complaints were passed on, that's where it ended," she said.

Lee said Vincent was viewed as 'untouchable'.

Face to face with my crotch? What a load of rubbish. For a start I'd have to be 6'8" for that to happen and I'm 5'7" but *The Canberra Times* couldn't even be bothered to use a tape measure in testing the veracity of what was always an outrageous fiction! From the time of her groundless complaint, she always made a point of turning her back to me.

The newspaper finally agreed that I had been defamed, paid a large sum by way of agreed reparations, and published the following apology on October 8, 2018.

Apology to Frank Vincent

On or about 20 January 2018 there appeared in the Saturday edition of *The Canberra Times* an article headed 'He was un-touchable' Radio Station 'failed on harassment complaints.'

The article contained an allegation of sexual assault against Mr Frank Vincent.

The Canberra Times accepts that the allegation referring to Mr Vincent is false.

The Canberra Times unreservedly withdraws the allegation against Mr Vincent and sincerely apologises to Mr Vincent for any hurt and embarrassment.

CHAPTER 17

A STROKE OF MISFORTUNE

I would stay in Canberra for another month after my dismissal. I hadn't even began unpacking boxes in my house at suburban O'Connor when I started re-filling those I had managed to empty.

I took some comfort from the fact my replacement would be dear friend Paul Holmes. I didn't begrudge him in any way, Holmesy had been down on his luck and if his lifeline was going to be the same rope used as my noose that would in some way reduce the burn on my neck. In fact, both chapters of my Canberra misadventures have been laced with serendipity – taking over the breakfast shift from my other great buddy and 2014 stand-in announcer Rob Duckworth, who had cleared the path for me to join Triple M more than 30 years earlier – and of course Holmsey had been crucial in my career's salvage by 2DayFM. So, what was *going* around was certainly *coming* around and rock solid friendships were not shaken for a second.

It's just as well I had my own stash of cash at the time as 2CA failed to deliver a promised $3000 severance cheque. So I sold a home I had purchased in Canberra and headed for the much more hospitable and warmer climes of Noosa on the Queensland Sunshine Coast. God knows I needed to thaw out – and chill-out after such a heavy ride. My exit from CA also freed me up to resume my broadcast liaison duties for HBS at the 2018 World Cup hosted by Russia. I arrived there only to discover the scandal had followed me in the form of an email to HBS' head of human resources. It contained a link to *The Canberra Times* article, and while she never revealed the sender's name the HR chief assured me all was ok. "We know you well Frank. We like you and we do not intend to replace you."

They were soothing words to say the least and I was soon back in the groove with HBS after 16 years as a reliable soldier for them. But talk about kicking a bloke when he is down.

To this day there has been no formal allegation about me tested by any tribunal or court but long after this sordid fantasy was created the mud still sticks.

It's timely now in my memoir to thank all those friends, relatives, past and present colleagues and listeners who have offered their unwavering support in challenging times. Not everyone subjected to such a vicious and vexatious campaign can survive the enormous, unrelenting stress of it – and if it were not for those champions who stood by me I can only speculate about how much heavier the psychological blows may have been. It's a long list of supporters who weighed-in behind me, as disbelieving as I was when hearing of the career wrecking claims.

My old mate from 2Day FM Mike Hammond and dear friend, Channel Nine sport journalist Tim Sheridan are prominent in my memory of those who rushed to my defence on social media, proudly announcing their unconditional support on Facebook. Mike, like Richard Wilkins, is a consummate all-rounder – mastering the arts of radio and television broadcasting as top rating announcer, voice over artist and TV personality – known to millions as the voice of Foxtel. I first met Tim through his wife Margaret Bates when she worked at Triple as our first female newsreader. A former Rugby player Tim was highly regarded for his beautifully scripted sports features on Nine's Wide World of Sports. He also presented sport on Nine's top rating news bulletins as deputy to Ken Sutcliffe. To have such highly respected fellow media personalities go into bat for the Black Rat meant the world to me. These were people I'd known for years, and they knew that these outrageous allegations from journalists – who didn't know me from a bar of soap – had to be countered with great force, and all the indignation their libellous muck deserved.

On the road to recovery with one of my carers, Sandy.

A change of scenery to the sub-tropical paradise of the Queensland Sunshine Coast was certainly a huge positive step away from the misery of Canberra.

I ended up buying a beautiful home at Sunrise Beach, and I began work at the local community radio station Noosa FM. Miki was travelling back and forth from The Netherlands and had also been extremely supportive despite our growing physical and emotional estrangement, caused no doubt by the extended time apart when I was in Canberra and she was busy with her career on the other side of the world. I guess the relationship was hanging on the gossamer thread of fading memories from the time of our full blown romance. She remained my closest friend, but we were more confidantes than lovers, a natural enough place for many couples to land I guess, but the sadness of failing to recapture our glory days was overwhelming at times and came with its own stresses.

The sudden, brutal exit from 2CA, my deteriorating marriage and the uncertainty about the future was certainly taking a serious toll on my physical well-being, and I started suffering mini seizures of dizziness, so bad that I would have to pull-over by the side of the road when driving and allow Miki to get behind the wheel. The dizziness would be accompanied by a sharp pain in my neck and jaw.

When I consulted a GP about these increasingly common episodes he didn't seem too concerned and tried to ease my mind. As I kicked back in a beautiful new home with magnificent shiny floorboards and a stunning swimming pool, all seemed well with my life – from the perspective of an outsider at least. Inside I was still restless, and yet to detoxify from the bitterness of the 2CA ordeal. The $50,000 settlement from the newspaper was a band aid of sorts, a meagre excuse for the bandaging actually needed for a haemorrhage of self-confidence and belief.

I felt like I had been punished for what more the flattering appraisals of my personality regarded as 'endearing eccentricity.' Others saw my quirks as something sinister and distasteful – having had their gullible minds poisoned by the profane publicity surrounding my professional demise. All these dark thoughts amounted to a nightly torture of tossing and turning, and blood pressure that was heading for the roof. We've all heard the expression: 'Doing my head in.' Never a truer word could have been said about the stresses I was suffering.

Along with millions of other Australian Rugby League supporters, I tuned in for the final game of the 2019 State of Origin. Although Queensland had secured the series it was a tense third game for a so called dead rubber and the Blues prevailed by just six points in the end to restore their morale ahead of the 2020 series.

The full time whistle had just been blown when I rose from the couch ton prepare for bed – and then without hitting any switch the lights had gone out. The only thing I was hitting was the deck of my living room floor.

I have very vague recollections of semi-conscious and lying face down in a puddle of my own vomit as my mobile phone almost rang itself flat the next morning with the persistent attempts of a friend to reach me. It turned out she had banging on the front door for an extended time after arriving to meet me for a morning swim. I could hear the phone but couldn't reach it on a coffee table because my body was paralysed, and particularly unresponsive on my left hand side. It was clear that something was seriously wrong and my friend's next call would be to Triple 0. The police ended up forcing entry to the home via a side door and they immediately called an ambulance.

So began a marathon that continues until this day.

I was later transferred to hospital where I would spend the next five months of my life. The same blood clot that had been causing my dizziness and jaw pain had blocked the blood supply to the right hand side of my brain, and I had suffered a serious stroke. But I was lucky to be alive. Had I not already arranged to go to the beach the morning after my collapse I shudder to think how long I would have been stricken on the floor without anyone raising an alarm.

With Miki still in The Netherlands and our marriage all but over my immediate family swung into action. Dad jumped on a plane to be at my bedside. What became known as Team Frank was locked into place for what was going to be a long and harrowing road ahead.

I had suffered what's known as an Ischaemic Stroke, occurring when the brain is denied the constant supply of oxygen and glucose delivered by the bloodstream. A blockage of more than a few minutes damages the region of the brain around the site of the clot and tissue begins to die. In my case the blockage was not cleared within a few hours, causing permanent brain damage. I can now use that as an excuse!

In becoming a medical statistic, I was staggered to learn I was one of 100 Australians suffering a stroke every day. I was lucky to be among the 85 percent of victims who will survive but I am among the 35 percent left with a permanent disability and just 10 percent requiring constant care.

The Australian Brain Foundation says: "A middle-aged man who has high blood pressure, high cholesterol, smokes and has uncontrolled diabetes increases his risk of stroke by *twenty* times."

Well, my blood pressure was certainly a decisive factor. It had skyrocketed from my happy decade in Amsterdam to be the most extreme it had ever been thanks to the mental cruelty inflicted by my colleagues and management at 2CA. I am in no doubt about that, and the ongoing attempts of that poisonous cohort to derail my relationship with Host Broadcast Services confirmed the true extent of the malice. If any of those malevolent people are reading this, then hang your heads in shame. You are a disgrace to the human race. Your conduct crosses the border of evil to remind us all that forces of darkness are never far away, ready to demoralise and dehumanise unwitting targets. I have worked with many sociopaths and narcissists in the media. It attracts them. But you lot win the prize, revelling in the misery inflicted on the victims of your gratuitous malice. You meet plenty of snakes in the reptilian swamp of the media but your blood runs *colder.* You sank your venom into my brain and almost killed me. It's when groundless libellous bile becomes criminal and should be investigated for a crime that's far more serious than mere malicious mischief. Their actions could have been considered homicidal if my swimming companion had not raised the alarm about what turned out to be my dying body.

An injection of blood thinners was the first emergency response at the hospital and almost certainly saved my life.

Since then, I've been constantly dwelling on the irony that by being near death I learned how to live. Yes, it been an ordeal but I've been determined to let my positive spirit prevail, and with the tremendous support of carers provided by the wonderful National Disability Insurance Scheme (NDIS), I have been able to start living all over again. There was one carer who was so supportive and conscientious. Her name was Katrina Smith – and I'd show my appreciation by nicknaming her 'Special K.'

I struggle with the powerful anti-seizure drugs from time to time. They can have a very negative impact physically and psychologically if the dosage isn't right, and as my recovery goes from strength to strength my medication has to be adjusted accordingly. For example, a neurologist has been engaged to regularly adjust my dosage, depending on how I'm travelling at any one time. My entire left side is super sensitive, and the stroke has reduced my slow walk to a limp. My skin is hypersensitive to the application of water. The ostensibly simple act of having a show can be extremely painful. A swim is out of the question. My mobility outside the home is totally dependent on my carers. At the time of writing I hadn't driven for five years. As a virtue of absolute necessity the passenger's seat has allowed me to literally slow down, and absorb so much more in moments of contemplation much quieter than those afforded by the madness of big city traffic.

I have taken a lot of inspiration from other stroke victims, who come from all corners of society. I was particularly encouraged by the words of famous Sydney restaurateur Peter Doyle, from his words penned for the Brain Foundation.

"It's been a hard road back ... my bloody oath it's been hard. Still is. You try undoing buttons and going to the toilet with one hand. You can't even do up a belt. Your lifestyle alters altogether, and you get so cranky with people.

And no matter how much money you've got, you can't buy your way out of it. Rich or poor, this thing can strike you down – there's no defining line in terms of wealth – or of age. After a stroke, you're buggered unless you've got someone to help you. I'm fortunate in having a retired merchant mariner, Pat Moss, to assist me. He's my driver, and pushes me in the wheelbarrow!"

It's that loss of independence to which Peter refers that really hits you hard.

For someone who once trotted the glove with impunity the impact a stroke has on one's minute *by minute* mobility can be crushing, and psychological supports become an integral part of the rehabilitation process to ensure your spirits don't dive towards a level of permanent depression. I was lucky to have an innately positive disposition before the stroke, and it has served me well in the darker moments. I must confront more than a few stark realities – including the fact I will never drive a car again. Some days I can get by without a cane to prop up my left side, and at times my limp can be so bad that I require a 'human walking stick' – someone I can put my right arm around to help me along the way. The left side of my body can also be extremely sensitive and painful to touch. Cold water pressure on my arm can be agonising.

I ended-up moving back to Sydney to be closer to family, and my nephew Vince Movizio was kind enough to offer me the use of his wonderful home – and he also proved to be a masterful motivator! Vince was a genuine Godsend – living proof that someone 'up there' really likes me after all. I woke one morning to hear Vince was piping recordings of my old 2CA breakfast shift through the house – and my mood lifted immediately in my surprise to remember just how brilliant I was! (Insert wink!) My speech started improving too, and many people have remarked that I'm starting to sound like my old self. It's one of the crueller twists to lose a voice on which you've depended so heavily to make a living. My voice was my passport. But in the weeks following the stroke I was sounding more like Forest Gump than the old Black Rat.

At this point it would be remiss of me not to pay a special tribute to my speech therapist Nuray Ozden. She worked wonders with my voice and over 18 months her expertise had me back sounding like the old Frank. When your voice is such a huge part of your identity, being able to sound like I once did would become a major building block in my recovery, and the restoration of enough confidence to confront the long list of other challenges. I can't thank her enough.

People often ask me if I miss have the odd social drink, but the thing I miss most apart from being able to drive myself around – is travel in the wider world. I loved every minute of my adventures abroad and look forward to the day when that can become a possibility once again. 40 countries is just not enough!

At the time of writing, I was looking to sell my Noosa home and resettle in a new house near my family in western Sydney, exactly where my amazing journey began.

CHAPTER 18

'THE PRICE OF AN EDUCATION'

When one-time Rolling Stones manager Allen Klein deftly snared the rights to the iconic band's pre-1971 recordings, including *Satisfaction* – guitarist Keith Richards was more philosophical than angry, insisting the expensive lessons in dealing with the slippery American businessmen were 'the price of an education.'

It was a typically cool Richards response to what may have incited rage in others, and in processing the pain inflicted on me in recent years I have been drawing a similar deep breath. I've often thought of Keith's attitude to the shrewd Klein in trying my best not to embittered by those who set out to destroy me as a pawn in their long game of gratuitous self-promotion.

So while Chapter 16 of this book had to be written to confront head-on the insidious, illegal and indelible destruction of my reputation these concluding words of reflection on a life lived large, hard and fast will dwell on the many years of joy I have been lucky enough to celebrate. I have thrived as a man in love, a survivor of bigotry and racism, an everywhere man who had the passion to chase dreams that seemed so elusive and lofty as I set out on this journey from the parched paving of suffocating suburbia.

Without blowing my own vuvuzela in a 'frank' appraisal of my adventures I have to say they have been truly unique. Not one broadcaster, of whom I aware at least, could possibly have replicated the bespoke twists and turns of my rollercoaster career. If such a person does exist in a parallel universe, then I will be prepared to be agnostic on the subject of extra-terrestrial life but – odds are – the pieces of my giant puzzle have not been mirrored and are unlikely to be reproduced to form an identical picture. For a start the pioneering days of FM radio in which I played my own part – can only happen once. The dominoes that fell after the finger flick from being an *Inflatable Sports Reporter* could only tumble along an inimitable path of a wholly improvised career.

But I'm still hoping the examples of self-belief from my story can be copied by future generations of aspiring broadcast journalists, as a playbook – if you like – on how sheer bloody and single mindedness will deliver results for anyone wanting to blast themselves out of any obscurity.

Doors won't open if you don't knock on them. Doors won't open if you don't barge into them with a shoulder. Doors won't open unless you kick them in. Doors won't open unless you pick the lock.

'Whatever it takes' of course should never be executed if that determination comes at a cost to others. I have always been quick to celebrate the importance of a collegiate attitude, even if the value I've placed on a team effort hasn't always been embraced or shared by all my colleagues along the way.

To say the media industry is competitive is somewhat tautologous I know. Axiomatic even. The competition between rival commercial outlets is a given, but from day to day it's more intense internally, and I'll quote Winston Churchill on that reality in his reference to where he found his most bitter adversaries.

"The opposition occupies the benches in front of you, but the enemy sits behind you."

And the wisdom of that other great wordsmith Eminem also resonated with me in penning my life story,

"The truth is you don't know what is going to happen tomorrow. Life is

a crazy ride, and nothing is guaranteed."

The rapper may not have had Churchill's eloquence but in the case of my life hardly a truer sequence of words could have been said.

But while Eminem's lyrics speak to a plain reality one can anticipate and prepare for the caprice of whatever the universe serves up on its daily menu. If you accept change as a given then you can navigate the stormiest of seas and most satisfying of big rolling waves as they propel one towards golden sands.

For me the stormy seas were churning thanks to the internecine and Machiavellian manoeuvring of giant egos within the management of the commercial media industry where the bottom line of profit was always present to determine one's ultimate fate. I've always been a fan of the maverick American journalist Hunter S Thompson, who could easily have been targeting all of the commercial media industry when he wrote about television.

"The TV business is uglier than most things. It is normally perceived as some kind of cruel and shallow money trench through the heart of the journalism industry, a long plastic hallway where thieves and pimps run free and good men die like dogs, for no good reason."

In the chapter *Capital Capers* I wasn't exactly glowing in my praise of Canberra, and my instincts should have guided me all along about the danger my career would crash into rocks within the environs of Australia's hotspot for political intrigue. Consistent with that prevailing theme, the politics of a local radio station would change my life forever despite my best intentions.

But in dissecting the importance of being Frank, it's equally vital to value an indomitable stance, the unwavering belief that the glass is always half full. Some might characterise such a powerful will to be positive in every circumstance as quixotic but as one who spent a large slice of my life in The Netherlands, I became accomplished at careering into windmills and getting straight back on that horse!

Don Quixote might have charged into the windmills of Spain but Holland, as the Netherlands has been informally known, provided me with plenty of practice with the 1000 windmills for which this low lying nation became so famous. So having referenced those Golden Sands earlier I'll extend the analogy to say Amsterdam was the most idyllic of my life's beaches. The city was the setting for the great love of my life and career opportunities that emerged due to the sheer force of my own never say die nature. The pursuit of one's passion should transcend any economic goals. The money will come but can't be a primary motivation in driving one's career in broadcast media. In my case a genuine love of football, basketball and motorsports provided a passport for the ultimate prize – spiritual fulfilment. And I'll cite Oscar Wilde again, this time in earnest.

"A cynic is a man who knows the price of everything, and the value of nothing."

The cynics in the media were the managers, and their mercantile masters. To sum them up I'll quote the great writer and humanitarian Charles Dickens in his description of the villainous Ralph Nickleby, the parsimonious uncle of Nicholas Nickleby, the hero of the novel bearing his name.

"Stern, unyielding, dogged, and impenetrable, Ralph cared for nothing in life, or beyond it, save the gratification of two passions, avarice, the first and predominant appetite of his nature, and hatred, the second."

I have met Ralph many times in the media, but always stared him down and turned on my heel to never hear the piece of coal that passes as his heart rattle again from its swing on a filthy piece of string.

I will isolate the trail blazing leaders of 2 Triple M as exceptions to the rule of ruthless bastardry in the executive suites. They were genuine pioneers – and *buccaneers* – sailing into an industry like pirates ready to sink the status quo of those who had it too good for too long. I was proud to sail under and salute Triple M's 'skull and crossbones' as the Mulray Bunch pillaged the loot of advertising dollars that would have been destined for the bulging pockets of the incumbent moguls.

But there have been far too many heroes on my journey to dwell for too long on the snipers who fired from the shadows, I have mentioned all those torch bearing, inspirational figures along the way but I want to list them in one place to make the final instalment of the enormous debt I owe them with a payment of the published acknowledgment they all so richly deserve.

Max Roley – the master mentor and custodian of Australian's golden tonsils who recommended me for my first announcing job at 2LT Lithgow.

The journos from *The Illawarra Mercury* – who became my friends and promoted my fledgling career as 2WL's 'elfin wunderkind' as I paid my dues on the graveyard shift.

Lee Jay Richards – the former 2SM announcer and 2WL music director who always had my interests at heart as I settled into the 'Gong.

Rob Duckworth – a great friend who has been unwaveringly supportive, and a colleague who steered me into my first capital city gig in Canberra before recommending me for breakthrough job at 2 Triple M.

Doug Mulray – the pioneering genius of the Australian airwaves who invited me into his all-conquering breakfast team and argued strongly for my retention when my enemies were circling. I miss him terribly.

David White – the Triple M News Director who showed me the

way in transitioning from radio announcing to broadcast news.

Allision Drower – a much loved Triple M colleague and MTV host, who has been extremely supportive throughout my career.

The Sydney Kings – the basketballers who took me on board as a virtual mascot in appreciation of my ongoing promotion of their franchise when the sport was struggling for mainstream media recognition.

Cherie Romero – for her integrity in preserving the myth my exit from Triple M was of my own design!

Paul Holmes – an incredibly loyal mate and colleague who smoothed the way for my employment at 2DayFM – and Brad March for making it all happen in the end.

Richard Wilkins – the *Today Show* veteran of entertainment reporting, always ready to give me such valuable advice.

Saul Shtien – the TV Sports executive who gave me my first break in television.

Bill Woods – one of the television industry's most talented and underrated over achievers, for his guidance in establishing my career as a motor racing journalist.

Miki Matsukawa – the great love of my life.

Garry Shaw – the production whiz from Host Broadcast Services who backed me in every time to maintain my role in the coverage for five World Cups.

And last but by no means least – my incredible family and carers for their support and belief through the best and worst of times.

Way back in Chapter 5 I mentioned how Roland Roll-a-door of *Roland Roll-a-door's Roll-a-doors* demanded he have the final say in this tale, and his infamous persuasive powers have persisted, so here it is – from the desk he shares with my old mate Dave Gibson.

"I've always seen eye to eye with Frank Vincent, and not just because we're both four feet tall. Before we actually met his fame preceded him. The rumour going around was that he had two penises. When I enquired as to why I was told: "Because you can't get that silly just playing with one."

But when we finally met outside of Triple M – because owing to a silly misunderstanding I was legally prohibited from getting within 100 metres of Doug Mulray – I found young Frankie to be a wise and erudite soul. For example, right away he saw the advantages of installing a Roland Roll-a-door Roll-a-door across the entrance to his garage as well as both the front and back entrances to his house. No need to go fumbling around his pockets for cumbersome metal keys. With just the press of a button he'd be off the street and into the bosom of lovely home. And speaking of bosoms, you've already read tales of the Black Rat's success with the ladies. But he's also honest enough to say that he's not always lucky in love. Truth be told, I've been to more Movizio weddings than I've had hot dinners (although to be fair, owing to a digestive complaint known as 'midget's colon' I can only manage room temperature food).

I tell you what, though- as you can tell by now The Rat has had a very interesting life. He's had his good times and bad. But the one thing I know about Franko Vincenzo Movizio is that no matter how many times he falls, as long as he lands on his head the little bastard will always bounce. And I'm telling you that for nothing!!

Roland Roll-a-door

With Lachy Doley after another sensational gig in Sydney, Live Instrumentalist of the Year 2016.

Special mentions

Ian Grace, Frank Mercuri, David White (Radio), Ron E Sparks, Dave Gibson, Peter Moon, Jeff Thomas.

Acknowledgements

Mark Evans, Wayne Fox, Simon Hicks, Melissa Hicks, Patrick DèWaad, Allison Drower, Helen Ziogertis, Ash Brenan, Jeremy Mather, Pete Armstrong, John Bell, Tim Sheriden, Mike Hammond, Richard Clapton, Lachy Doley, Catherine Swinton, Paul Campion, Daryl Missen, Jeff Thomas, Piera Thomas, Wayne Fox, Peter Cusato, Daye Cusato, Keith Cusato, Lisa Olsen, Lisa Charlwood, Katrina Smith, Lindy East, John Andriano, Morrie Cantarella, Vicki Pollard, Ron Pollard, Tim Morrissey, Damian Keogh, Bob Turner, Bob Gallagher, Mark Viduka, Pekka Kaidesoja, Adrian Atkinson, Jyrki Kempainen, Wayne Daykin, Neil Wright, Adrian Johnston, Geoff Phillips, Michelle Tydd, Michelle Becroft.

As told to Adam Walters

With special thanks to Mike Colman for his contribution to Chapter 9 (Barcelona)

First published in 2024 by New Holland Publishers
Sydney

Level 1, 178 Fox Valley Road, Wahroonga, NSW 2076, Australia

newhollandpublishers.com

A record of this book is held at the National Library of Australia.

ISBN 9781760796068

Managing Director: Fiona Schultz
Project Editor: Xavier Waterkeyn
Designer: Andrew Davies
Production Director: Arlene Gippert
Printed in China

10 9 8 7 6 5 4 3 2 1

Keep up with New Holland Publishers:
NewHollandPublishers
@newhollandpublishers